BEGINNER'S GUIDE TO
WINNING CHESS

249 FOLLOW-THE-PLAY DIAGRAMS
11 SYSTEMATIC REVIEW TESTS *with*
350 SIMPLIFIED QUESTIONS AND ANSWERS

Fred Reinfeld, the famous chess authority, has now written the finest book ever done on chess for beginners. Adapting the latest question-and-answer techniques to the royal game, he demonstrates how chess can be absorbed easily by anyone who will follow his guidance.

His book begins with the basic rules and with diagrams that illustrate, step by step, the moving and capturing powers of each piece. Immediately, Mr. Reinfeld poses a series of questions through which you can review what you have learned and, thus, reinforce the quantity, as well as the quality, of your learning. Eleven such systematic "Review Tests" are interspersed throughout the text with the answers in each instance given nearby so that you can check them out quickly.

In Chapter II, the author explains the standard system of chess notation so that you can follow printed games anywhere, in newspapers, journals, or in anthologies of games by the masters.

Chapter III is given to "The Art of Checkmate." The follow-the-play diagrams offer simple but typical examples to help you grasp the logic of each move and to encourage you to start playing your own first game.

In Chapter IV, "How to Win Material," you learn about the different modes of attack, such as fork and pins. In Chapter V, "Superior Force Wins: Simple Endgames," you learn how to move to victory in basic endgames. Here, too, you go from move to

move with the author to guide you.

In Chapter VI, you absorb the "Principles of Opening Play." You have already learned how the chessmen operate, how they attack, defend, threaten, win material, and give checkmate. Now you learn "how they get that way," or how you can move them into position with maximum power, how to menace the enemy's forces, and how to protect your own.

In Chapter VII, "Some Model Openings," the author leads you into the development of standard openings that you can use for your basic ideas and for winning play.

In Chapter VIII, Mr. Reinfeld offers complete games as an organic process of opening, middlegame, and endgame conclusions. He appraises the opening moves and their likely consequences, and shows how the early jockeying for advantage can lead you either to success or to failure. As he puts it, "Each game is a kind of sermon which preaches the virtues of effective development and denounces the defects of bad development."

What is most remarkable about this new book is that with the 350 questions and answers Mr. Reinfeld has provided a guide to winning chess not only for the tyro but also for the more experienced player. Anyone who has ever dreamt of playing chess and winning at it will profit from this book. *Beginner's Guide to Winning Chess* is an investment in years of pleasure.

ABOUT THE AUTHOR

Fred Reinfeld is, as Dr. M. W. Sullivan states in his introduction to *Beginner's Guide to Winning Chess*, a brilliant chess player and "the leading writer on chess in the entire history of the game." This is indeed saying a great deal, since chess has been played for better than a thousand years, but the overwhelming evidence is that the Sullivan statement is actually true!

In individual tournament encounters, Mr. Reinfeld has defeated such outstanding champions as Frank Marshall, Samuel Reshevsky, Arnold Denker, Reuben Fine, and I. A. Horowitz. He has himself won the New York state championship, the Manhattan Chess Club championship, and the Marshall Chess Club championship.

As a chess authority, he has produced volumes that have been instructive as well as delightful for sheer clarity. He was for many years Associate Editor of *Chess Review*. He earned wide acclaim for his chess courses at the School of General Education at New York University. In recent years he has been associated with leaders in the field of programmed teaching. While counseling with them in the development of revolutionary new techniques for chess instruction he evolved the special presentation on which *Beginner's Guide to Winning Chess* is based.

With his inquiring mind, his gift for language, and his astonishing grasp of whole new subjects, it would be surprising if Fred Reinfeld did not lend his talents to other fields. He has done so with astonishing results. He cannot say readily how many books he has written, in biography, in general history for children as well as for adults, on natural science, on stamp collecting, on coin collecting, etc. Every new topic is a challenge to him and is likely to be the seed for a new and charmingly written book. But chess is his first love, and in *Beginner's Guide to Winning Chess* he has produced a work that will prove to be his best guide for the new chess player. Certainly it is a landmark in chess literature.

BEGINNER'S GUIDE
to WINNING CHESS

FRED REINFELD

Melvin Powers
Wilshire Book Company

12015 Sherman Road, No. Hollywood, CA 91605

**Published by arrangement with
Follett Publishing Company.**

Copyright © 1964 by Fred Reinfeld.
All rights reserved. No portion of this book may be
reproduced in any form without written permission
of the publisher.
Manufactured in the United States of America

Library of Congress Catalog Card Number 64-14258

ISBN 0-87980-215-4

CONTENTS

INTRODUCTION

Ours is no age for a universal genius, but Fred Reinfeld offers us a close approximation of the ideal. The quality and quantity of his books make him not only the finest chess author of our day, but also the leading writer on chess in the entire history of the game.

Of course, Fred Reinfeld was, and is, a brilliant chess player. But many of the game's greatest players have proved nothing less than unintelligible when they tried to communicate their secrets through the medium of the printed page. Reinfeld, on the other hand, has been as great a writer as he has been a chess player. Furthermore, whether writing on natural science, whaling, coin collecting, stamp collecting or general biography for children or adults, he has employed that elegant yet forceful style that demonstrates his fine command of the English language as well as of the subject in hand.

Naturally, Reinfeld's paramount interest as a dedicated chess authority has been in how people learn to play chess and how more people could be attracted to this international game. His teaching experience has run the entire gamut from lecturing on chess to college students to finding ways to teach the moves to five-year-olds. His own writings improved as he learned more and more about what and how much material could be taught and how it should be presented at any given stage. It is this constant and creative experimentation in chess education that prepared him to write a truly great book for beginners. Like many of his readers, I often urged him to prepare a volume which would offer a concise but complete statement of what he considers the essentials of the game. I realized that it would be no mean task to encompass within a single book the knowledge gained from forty years of teaching chess, but I thought that if anyone could do it, it would be Fred Reinfeld.

In *Beginner's Guide to Winning Chess,* Reinfeld has succeeded brilliantly in constructing a text which serves both as a complete treatment of the game, from the beginner's point of view, and as a reference for the more advanced player. After a thorough discussion of the rules of the game, this book gives a simple and clear explanation of chess notation and of the relative values of the pieces. The student then learns the basic types of checkmate, so that he will be goal-oriented when he finally does begin to play. There follows a section designed to teach the beginner how to win material in the mid-game. Reinfeld proceeds to the best elementary treatment of the endgame I have ever seen. He then examines opening strategy and tactics in a way that offers the novice an excellent chance to find out *why* he is making opening moves, rather than mechanically following memorized variations. Finally, after a critical examination of some model openings, he gives the student a chance to pit himself against the masters in some lively and well-annotated games.

Most important of all, eleven precise and comprehensive review tests are included within the body of the work. The student of chess has an opportunity to evaluate his progress by determining immediately how well he has understood each step.

In summation, I can only say that this is the most concise yet comprehensive treatment of the game of chess ever written. I recommend it without reservation to the chess-playing public.

M. W. Sullivan, Ph.D.
Los Altos, California

CHAPTER I

BASIC RULES

CHESS is a game played by two opponents who are always referred to as "White" and "Black."

White always makes the first move. Thereafter the players take turns in making their moves.

THE CHESSBOARD AND CHESSMEN

Play takes place on a board made up of 64 squares arranged in eight vertical rows and eight horizontal rows. See Diagram 1.

The squares are alternately colored light and dark. Regardless of their actual colors, the light squares are always called "white" and the dark squares are always called "black."

The horizontal rows of squares—running from side to side—are called "ranks."

The vertical rows—running "north" and "south" in the diagrams—are called "files."

There are also rows of squares known as "diagonals." These are made up of squares of the same color and touch only at the corners.

Before setting up the chessmen in the opening position, place the board so that the right-hand corner square nearest each player is a *white* square.

Diagram 1
BLACK

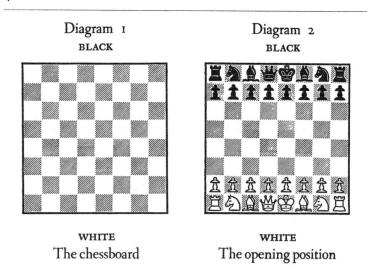

WHITE
The chessboard

Diagram 2
BLACK

WHITE
The opening position

Each player starts with 16 chessmen. White has light-colored men and Black has dark-colored men.

White sets up his men, the white forces, on the two ranks nearest him, as in Diagram 2. Black also sets up his men, the black forces, on his two nearest ranks (Diagram 2).

Each player has six different kinds of men. Here are their symbols:

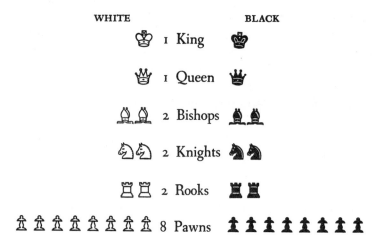

WHITE		BLACK
♔	1 King	♚
♕	1 Queen	♛
♗ ♗	2 Bishops	♝ ♝
♘ ♘	2 Knights	♞ ♞
♖ ♖	2 Rooks	♜ ♜
♙ ♙ ♙ ♙ ♙ ♙ ♙	8 Pawns	♟ ♟ ♟ ♟ ♟ ♟ ♟

The chessmen are divided into two classes. One consists of the Pawns; the other is made up of all the remaining men. A King or Knight, for example, is a "piece." But a Pawn is simply a Pawn.

The most important chessman is the King, because the object of the game is to attack the King in such a way that he cannot escape capture. This is known as "checkmate," and the King is said to be "checkmated." The player who has brought about the checkmate is the winner.

Striving for checkmate must always be uppermost in the thoughts and intentions of both players. We shall, therefore, have a great deal to say about it later on. But first we must learn how the chessmen move and capture, after noting how they are posted at the beginning of the game.

Each player places his pieces on his first rank—the rank nearest him. See Diagram 2.

There is a way of distinguishing between each of the two Rooks, Knights, and Bishops. Again referring to Diagram 2, observe that the Rook, Knight, and Bishop nearest the King are known respectively as the King Rook, King Knight, and King Bishop. Similarly, the Rook, Knight, and Bishop nearest the Queen are known respectively as the Queen Rook, Queen Knight, and Queen Bishop.

The Rooks look like medieval towers or castles, and for this reason the piece is sometimes called a "Castle." Each Rook is placed on a corner square of the first rank.

An interesting point to note here is that each file is named for the piece which is placed on it at the beginning of the game. Thus, the file at White's extreme right on which the King Rook is placed is known as the "King Rook file." The file on which the Queen Rook is placed, at White's extreme left, is known as the "Queen Rook file."

The Knight is easy to identify, as it always is given the form of a horse's head. The Knights are placed one square in, next to the Rooks. The King Knight is on the King Knight file; the Queen Knight is on the Queen Knight file.

The top of the Bishop has a cleft which makes it look like a bishop's miter. The Bishops are placed next to the Knights, one square nearer to the middle of the first rank. The King Bishop (next to the King) goes on the King Bishop file; the Queen Bishop, on the Queen Bishop file.

Now we have to place the King and Queen on the two middle squares of the first rank. The Queen is the second tallest piece. Her diagram symbol is a spiked crown or coronet.

The placement of the Queen is governed by the rule of "Queen on color." This means that a White Queen is placed on the white middle square of White's first rank. The Black Queen is placed on the black middle square of Black's first rank.

Both Queens face each other across the Queen file. See Diagram 2.

The King is the tallest piece. His diagram symbol is a crown topped by a small cross. Each King is placed next to the Queen on the remaining empty square of the first rank.

The Kings face each other across the King file. See Diagram 2.

The placement of the Pawns is easy. On both sides the Pawns are placed on the second ranks, directly in front of the pieces. Check this on Diagram 2.

Each Pawn has its own special name—also a very simple matter. A Pawn is named after the piece which stands in back of it at the beginning of the game. We can describe the same fact in another way: each Pawn is named for the file on which it is placed.

Example: The Pawn in front of the Queen—on the Queen file—is called the "Queen Pawn." The Pawn in front of the King Knight—on the King Knight file—is called the "King Knight Pawn."

FIRST REVIEW TEST
(answers on page 8)

1. The two players in a game of chess are known as _____ (color) and _____(color).

2. _____(color) always makes the first move.

3. The chessboard is made up of _____(number) squares.

4. There are _____(number) horizontal rows, known as _____.

5. There are _____(number) vertical rows, known as _____.

6. A diagonal is a row of squares of the _____ color which touch only at their _____.

7. The squares of the chessboard are alternately colored _____ and _____.

8. The board is placed so that the right-hand corner square nearest each player is _____(color).

9. Each player starts with _____(number) chessmen.

10. The _____ is the most important chessman.

11. The object of the game is to _____ the opposing King.

12. When a King is attacked and cannot escape, he is said to be _____.

13. Each player posts his pieces on his _____(number) rank at the beginning of the game.

14. Each player posts his _____ on his second rank at the beginning of the game.

15. The _____ go in the corner squares at the beginning of the game.

16. The symbol for a Rook (is/is not) a horse's head.

17. The diagram symbol for the _____ is a crown with a small cross on top.

18. The Bishop nearest the King is called the _____ _____.

19. A file is named for the _____ which is placed on it at the beginning of the game.

20. The file on which the King Knight is placed is called the _____ _____ file.

21. At the beginning of the game the Black Queen is placed on a _____(color) square.

22. In the opening position the Pawn in front of the King Rook is called the _____ _____ Pawn.

First Review Test: Answers

1. White; Black	12. checkmated
2. White	13. first
3. 64	14. Pawns
4. 8; ranks	15. Rooks
5. 8; files	16. is not
6. same; corners	17. King
7. light; dark	18. King Bishop
8. white	19. piece
9. 16	20. King Knight
10. King	21. black
11. checkmate	22. King Rook

HOW THE CHESSMEN MOVE AND CAPTURE

Each chessman has its own distinctive way of moving and capturing. Before we study each of these ways, we need some general information about moves.

Only one move can be made at a time.

Only one chessman can be moved at a time. (There is one exception to this, known as "castling," which involves a combined move of King and Rook. See pages 23-26.)

When a chessman has been moved from one square to another square, the move is completed.

Only one chessman can occupy a given square at a time.

All chessmen, with the single exception of the Knight, move in only one direction at a time.

No chessman, again with the single exception of the Knight, can jump or leap over other chessmen.

All pieces capture in the same way that they move. The Pawn's way of moving, however, differs from its way of capturing.

A chessman captures an enemy chessman by replacing it on its square. The captured man is removed from its square and replaced by the capturing chessman. Diagrams 4 and 5 show how this is done.

The King

The King can move one square in any direction—horizontally, vertically, or diagonally. The crosses in Diagram 3 denote squares to which the King can move.

Diagram 3
BLACK

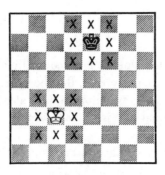

WHITE

How the King moves

Diagram 4
BLACK

WHITE

Before capturing

Diagram 5
BLACK

WHITE

After capturing

Note: The King can never make a move or a capture which will put him inside the capturing range of an enemy chessman.

The King captures the same way that he moves—one square in any direction. Thus, in Diagram 4 the White King can capture the Black Pawn or the Black Bishop. Diagram 5 shows the position after the King has captured the Pawn.

The Queen

Like the King, the Queen also moves in all directions—horizontally, vertically, or diagonally. But the Queen has an enormous range; she can reach any empty square along an unobstructed file, rank, or diagonal that is available from the square on which she is placed.

At best, the Queen can have a maximum of 27 possible squares to move to. This is shown in Diagram 6 where the Queen can move to *any* square marked with a cross.

Diagram 6

BLACK

WHITE

How the Queen moves

This enormous range makes the Queen the most powerful piece on the board.

The Queen captures in the same manner that she moves. In Diagram 7 she has a choice of capturing the Black Rook or the Black Knight. However, she cannot capture the Black Pawn, since her path along the diagonal is blocked by the White Pawn.

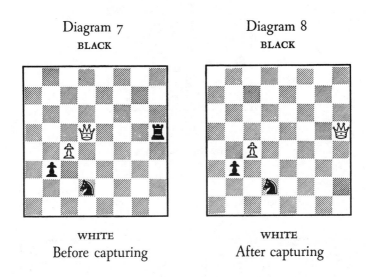

Diagram 7
BLACK

Diagram 8
BLACK

WHITE
Before capturing

WHITE
After capturing

Diagram 8 shows the position resulting from the Queen's capture of the Black Rook.

The Rook

The Rook is the most powerful piece after the Queen. It can move horizontally or vertically. The crosses in Diagram 9 show the possible squares to which the Rook can move.

In Diagram 10 White's Rook has the choice of capturing the Black Bishop or the Black Pawn. But the Rook cannot capture the Black Knight because the White Pawn blocks the path. Also note that the Rook cannot capture the Black Queen because the Rook cannot move on a diagonal.

Diagram 11 shows the position after the White Rook captures the Black Bishop.

Diagram 9

BLACK

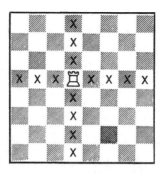

WHITE

How the Rook moves

Diagram 10

BLACK

WHITE

Before capturing

Diagram 11

BLACK

WHITE

After capturing

The Bishop

The Bishop is not quite so powerful as the Rook. The Bishop moves diagonally, always on squares of the same color. At the beginning of the game one Bishop is placed on a white square

Diagram 12
BLACK

WHITE
How the Bishop moves

and can move only on white squares for the rest of the game. The other Bishop is placed on a black square—check this on Diagram 2—and can move only on black squares for the balance of the game.

In Diagram 12 the Black Bishop can move to any square marked with a cross. The Bishop can move to any square on any

Diagram 13
BLACK

WHITE
Before capturing

Diagram 14
BLACK

WHITE
After capturing

unobstructed diagonal on which he happens to be located.

The Bishop captures in the same way that he moves. In Diagram 13 the Black Bishop can capture any of the White Pawns. However, the Bishop cannot capture the White Knight, as the path is blocked by the Black Rook.

Diagram 14 shows the position resulting from a capture of one of the Pawns.

The Knight

The Knight's move has some interesting aspects.

The Knight, for example, is the only chessman that can leap over other men, friendly or hostile.

In addition, it is the only chessman that does not move on a line.

In effect, the Knight moves two squares—first one square sideways or up or down, and then one square diagonally, still moving away from the square on which it started its move.

Thus, in Diagram 15 the Black Knight has a choice of eight possible moves, indicated by crosses. All these moves are of the same length.

Diagram 15

BLACK

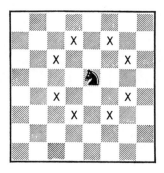

WHITE

How the Knight moves

Note that the Knight always changes the color of his square in moving. If he moves from a white square, he ends up on a black square. If he moves from a black square, he ends up on a white square.

Regarding the Knight's capturing powers, observe that he captures *only on the end-square of his move.* He can leap over friendly or hostile men to reach his end-square, but he cannot capture any of the enemy men on the intervening squares.

In Diagram 16, for example, the White Knight can capture any one of the Black Pawns. The presence of the White Queen and Black Rook does not affect the capturing possibilities in any way.

Diagram 17 shows the situation resulting from the capture of a Black Pawn.

Diagram 16
BLACK

Diagram 17
BLACK

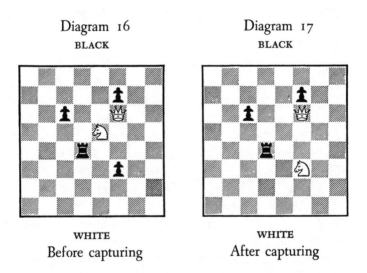

WHITE
Before capturing

WHITE
After capturing

SECOND REVIEW TEST
(answers on page 17)

1. Each chessman (has/does not have) its own distinctive way of moving and capturing.
2. There is one exception to the rule that only one chessman

can be moved at a time. This exception is known as
_____.

3. How many chessmen can occupy a given square at a time?
4. The only chessman that moves in more than one direction at a time is the _____.
5. The _____ is the only chessman that can leap or jump over the other chessmen.
6. The _____ is the only chessman that has a way of capturing which differs from the way in which it moves.
7. A chessman _____ an enemy chessman by replacing it on its square.
8. The King (can/cannot) move one square in any direction.
9. The King (can/cannot) move inside the capturing range of an enemy chessman.
10. The King (captures/does not capture) the same way that he moves.
11. [Diagram 4] The White King (can/cannot) capture the Black Pawn or the Black Bishop.
12. The Queen can move horizontally, vertically, or _____.
13. The _____ is the most valuable chessman.
14. The _____ is the most powerful chessman.
15. The White Queen (can/cannot) capture the Black Pawn when in the position shown in Diagram 7. Reason?
16. The _____ moves horizontally or vertically.
17. [Diagram 10] The White Rook (can/cannot) capture the Black Queen. Reason?
18. The _____ moves diagonally, always on squares of the same color.
19. [Diagram 13] The Black Bishop (can/cannot) capture the White Knight. Reason?
20. The _____ is the only piece that always makes a move of uniform length (aside from the King).
21. If a Knight moves from a white square, he lands on a _____(color) square.
22. The Knight (can/cannot) capture enemy men on the intervening squares of his move.
23. [Diagram 16] The White Knight has a choice of capturing

any one of _____(number) Black Pawns.

24. [Diagram 16] The White Knight (can/cannot) leap over the White Queen.

25. [Diagram 16] The White Knight (can/cannot) capture the Black Rook.

Second Review Test: Answers

1. has
2. castling
3. one
4. Knight
5. Knight
6. Pawn
7. captures
8. can
9. cannot
10. captures
11. can
12. diagonally
13. King
14. Queen

15. cannot; the diagonal is blocked by the White Pawn
16. Rook
17. cannot; the Rook does not move diagonally
18. Bishop
19. cannot; the diagonal is blocked by the Black Rook
20. Knight
21. black
22. cannot
23. three
24. can
25. cannot

The Pawn

Though the Pawn is the weakest of all the chessmen, it plays a vital role in the game. Inexperienced players have little respect for the Pawn, but they would do well to heed the slogan: Never underestimate the power of a Pawn!

The Pawn has at least four interesting qualities that set it apart from the pieces. These are:

1. The Pawn is the only chessman that moves in only one direction.

2. The Pawn is the only chessman that captures in a manner different from the way in which it moves.

3. The Pawn is the only chessman that can be converted into a unit of vastly enhanced power.

4. The Pawn is the only chessman that can capture *en passant* ("in passing").

The Pawn can move straight ahead—and only straight ahead—one square at a time.

White Pawns move forward from the White side toward the Black side. (That is, up the page or up the diagram.) Black Pawns move in the opposite direction. (Down the page or down the diagram.)

Each diagram is captioned BLACK at the top and WHITE at the bottom. This gives you the direction in which the Pawns move: Black Pawns *toward* the White side, White Pawns *toward* the Black side.

Diagrams 18 and 19 illustrate these points.

There is one important exception to the one-square advance of the Pawn. Any Pawn that is still on its original square (as in Diagram 2) has the option of advancing either one square *or* two, in one move.

Diagram 18
BLACK

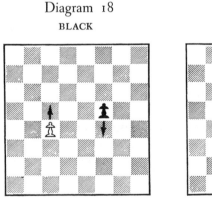

WHITE
Before the Pawns move

Diagram 19
BLACK

WHITE
After the Pawns
have moved

After the Pawn has exercised the option or refused it, one-square advances become the rule with no further exceptions.

Starting from the opening position (Diagram 2), let us examine the two types of initial Pawn moves.

Assume that White advances his King Pawn *two squares* (exercising the option) and Black replies by advancing his King Pawn *one square* (declining the option). The resulting situation is shown in Diagram 20.

Now, for his second move, White advances his Queen Pawn *two squares* (again exercising the option) and Black replies by advancing his Queen Pawn two squares (also exercising the option). This gives us the situation shown in Diagram 21.

Diagram 20
BLACK

WHITE
After White's and Black's first moves

Diagram 21
BLACK

WHITE
After White's and Black's second moves

As already pointed out, the Pawn's way of capturing differs from its way of moving. It moves one square straight ahead. It captures one square *diagonally* ahead, to the right or left.

In Diagram 22 the White Pawn on the left has the choice of capturing the Black Rook or Knight. The Black Pawn on the right has the choice of capturing the White Queen or Bishop. The White and Black Pawns in the central area cannot capture each other; they merely block each other's further advance.

Diagram 23 shows the situation after White's Pawn has captured the Black Rook and Black's Pawn has captured the White Queen. The Pawns in the center still continue to block each other.

Diagram 22   Diagram 23
BLACK   BLACK

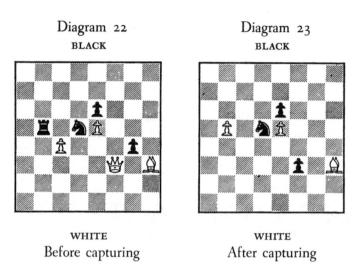

WHITE   WHITE
Before capturing   After capturing

Capturing En Passant

Pawns capture Pawns in the same way that they capture pieces; the attacking Pawn moves one square diagonally forward. In other words, when a Pawn captures a Pawn, it moves to an adjacent file on the left or right.

Now consider the following situation. In Diagram 24 White has a Pawn on his fifth rank (count five ranks from White's side of the board). Black has a Pawn on his second rank (count two ranks from Black's side of the board) on a file adjacent to the White Pawn.

Assume it is Black's move and he advances his Pawn one square. This gives us the position shown in Diagram 25. White's Pawn can now capture Black's Pawn according to rule, producing the position shown in Diagram 27.

Now return to Diagram 24. It is Black's move. He advances

Diagram 24
BLACK

WHITE

White's Pawn is on its fifth rank; the hostile Pawn is on its second rank on an adjacent file

Diagram 25
BLACK

WHITE

Black's Pawn has advanced from its second to its third rank. White can now capture according to rule

his Pawn two squares and produces the position pictured in Diagram 26.

Diagram 26
BLACK

WHITE

Black has advanced his Pawn two squares

Diagram 27
BLACK

WHITE

White has captured the Black Pawn

White now has the option of capturing *en passant* (in passing). He can capture the Black Pawn *as if it had advanced only one square,* and this capture in passing again leads to the situation shown in Diagram 27.

White does not *have* to capture in passing. But if he is to do it, he must do it in reply to the two-square advance of Black's Pawn. If he does not capture in passing in reply, he loses his option to do so.

Naturally Black has the same option to capture if the situation is reversed; that is, if White has a Pawn on his second rank while Black has a Pawn on his fifth rank on an adjoining file. If White now advances his Pawn two squares, Black can capture in passing.

Though capturing in passing is optional, there are two exceptional situations in which a player loses this right of choice:

First, if an *en passant* capture would expose the capturing player's King to attack, then he cannot capture in passing.

Second, if an *en passant* capture is the only way the player can get his King out of attack, then that capture *must* be made.

Pawn Promotion

This is a potential power possessed by the Pawn which enormously increases its value. When a Pawn reaches the last or eighth rank—all the way at the farther end of its file—it must be replaced by a Queen or Rook or Bishop or Knight of the same color.

In actual practice a Queen is almost always selected, as this is the most powerful piece on the board. It does not matter whether or not the player still possesses his original Queen or whatever other piece he is promoting to. Theoretically a player could have nine Queens—his original one and eight acquired through promotion. Later on we shall see that the possibility of "queening" a Pawn is of enormous importance.

Now for the actual mechanics of promoting a Pawn. In Diagram 28 a White Pawn and a Black Pawn are poised to queen. Both are just about to move on to the queening square on the last rank.

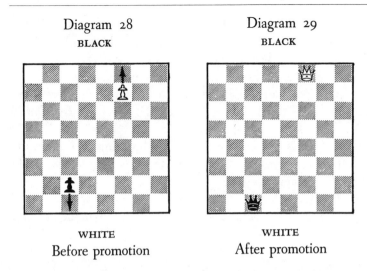

Diagram 28
BLACK

Diagram 29
BLACK

WHITE
Before promotion

WHITE
After promotion

White's Pawn advanced to his eighth rank and was promoted to (replaced by) a White Queen. Black's Pawn advanced to his eighth rank and was promoted to (replaced by) a Black Queen. See Diagram 29.

CASTLING

This very special move has been left for the end of our study describing the moves of the chessmen. Castling is played with the object of getting the King to a reasonably safe refuge at the side of the board. (To keep the King in the center would be courting disaster.)

Castling is the only move in chess which involves the movement of two pieces—the King and one of the Rooks.

There are many restrictions on castling. Even when it is possible, it can only be played once in a game by each player.

The two methods of castling are King-side castling (with the King Rook) and Queen-side castling (with the Queen Rook).

In King-side castling White moves his King two squares to the right and then places his King Rook to the immediate left of the King's new position.

Black castles King-side by moving his King two squares to the left and then placing his King Rook to the immediate right of the King's new position. (This is viewing the situation from Black's side of the board.) See Diagrams 30 and 31.

Castling Queen-side—with the Queen Rook—involves the same principle, but the mechanics are somewhat different because there are *three* squares between the King and the Queen Rook.

White castles Queen-side by moving his King two squares to the left and then placing his Queen Rook to the immediate right of the King's new position.

Black castles Queen-side by moving his King two squares to the right and then placing his Queen Rook to the immediate left

Diagram 30

BLACK

WHITE

Before castling

of the King's new position. (Once more, remember that this is viewing the situation from Black's side of the board.) See Diagram 32.

Some restrictions on castling are permanent. Once they appear, it becomes impossible for the rest of the game.

Other restrictions are temporary. When these restrictive conditions disappear at some later point in the game, it becomes possible to castle.

As for the permanent restrictions, if a player has moved his

Diagram 31
BLACK

WHITE
After King-side
castling

Diagram 32
BLACK

WHITE
After Queen-side
castling

King, he is permanently deprived of the opportunity to castle.
See Diagram 33.

If a player has moved his King Rook, he cannot castle King-side, but he may be able to castle Queen-side.

If a player has moved his Queen Rook, he cannot castle Queen-

Diagram 33
BLACK

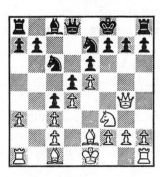

WHITE
White can castle; Black
cannot

Diagram 34
BLACK

WHITE
White cannot castle;
Black can

side, but he may be able to castle King-side. See Diagram 34 where White has moved both Rooks.

Of course, the loss of either Rook would also prohibit castling with it.

Here are the temporary restrictions on castling:

1. If a player's King is attacked ("in check"), he cannot castle.

2. If a square between a player's King and one of his Rooks is occupied, he cannot castle with that Rook.

3. If, in order to castle, a player has to move his King over a square controlled by an enemy chessman, he cannot castle. (This restriction does not apply to a castling Rook.)

4. If castling would result in placing the King on a square controlled by an enemy chessman, then castling is impossible.

Remember that castling becomes possible once these conditions are removed.

THIRD REVIEW TEST
(answers on pages 28–29)

1. The _____ is the only chessman that moves in only one direction.
2. White Pawns move toward the _____(color) side.
3. The Pawn (moves/does not move) straight ahead.
4. On its first move at any time during a game, a Pawn (has/does not have) the option of moving one square or two squares straight ahead.
5. The Pawn (can/cannot) move backward.
6. The King Bishop Pawn is the Pawn placed on the _____ _____ file.
7. The Pawn captures one square _____ ahead.
8. A White Pawn placed on White's third rank (can/cannot) capture a Black Pawn placed on Black's fifth rank on the same file.
9. A Pawn can capture only a _____ in passing.
10. A Pawn can capture in passing only if it is placed on its _____(number) rank.

11. A Pawn can be captured in passing if it has just moved from its _____(number) rank to its _____ (number) rank.

12. When a Pawn is captured in passing, the effect is the same as if it had moved to its _____(number) rank.

13. If a player does not immediately exercise his option to capture in passing, he (can/cannot) capture the same Pawn in passing later in the game.

14. If a capture in passing would expose a player's King to attack, then he (can/cannot) capture in passing.

15. If a capture in passing is the only way to get a King out of attack, then that capture (must/must not) be made.

16. When a Pawn reaches the eighth rank, it must be replaced by a _____ or _____ or or _____ of the same color.

17. In actual practice a Pawn is usually promoted to a _____.

18. A player (can/cannot) have more than one Queen.

19. Castling is a combined move of the _____ and a _____.

20. King-side castling takes place with the King Rook, while Queen-side castling takes place with the _____ _____.

21. In castling, the King moves _____(number) squares toward the Rook with which castling is to take place.

Diagram 35

BLACK

WHITE *to move*

Diagram 36

BLACK *to move*

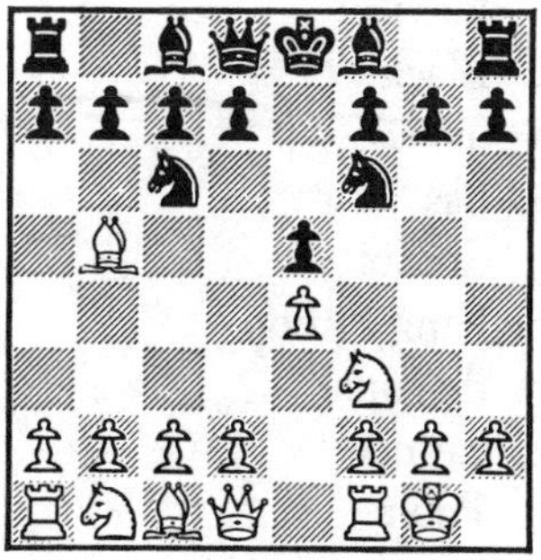

WHITE

22. If the King has moved, castling (is/is not) possible.
23. If the King Rook has moved, castling with that Rook (is/is not) possible.
24. [Diagram 35] White (can/cannot) castle. Reason?
25. [Diagram 36] Black (can/cannot) castle. Reason?
26. [Diagram 37] White (can/cannot) castle. Reason?
27. [Diagram 38] Black (can/cannot) castle. Reason?

Diagram 37
BLACK

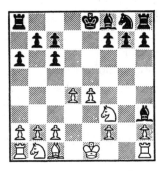

WHITE *to play*

Diagram 38
BLACK *to move*

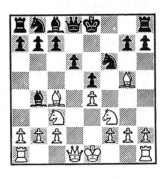

WHITE

Third Review Test: Answers

1. Pawn
2. Black
3. moves
4. has
5. cannot
6. King Bishop
7. diagonally
8. cannot
9. Pawn
10. fifth
11. second; fourth
12. third
13. cannot
14. cannot
15. must
16. Queen; Rook; Bishop; Knight
17. Queen
18. can
19. King; Rook
20. Queen Rook
21. two

22. is not
23. is not
24. cannot; his King is in check
25. cannot; one of the squares between King and King Rook is occupied
26. cannot; the White King cannot pass over the square controlled by Black's Queen Bishop
27. cannot; castling would place Black's King inside the capturing range of White's King Bishop.

CHECK AND CHECKMATE

We have seen earlier that the basic way to win a game of chess is to checkmate the opposing King—that is, to attack the King in such a way that he cannot escape.

Any attack on the King is called a "check." When a player's King is checked, he must try to get his King out of check—in other words, try to put an end to the attack. There are three ways in which he can do this:

1. By capturing the hostile chessman that is giving the check.
2. By moving his King off the line of attack.
3. By placing ("interposing") one of his men between his King and the hostile chessman that is giving check.

If the check can be removed, the game goes on. If there is no way of getting out of check, then the King is checkmated.

Note: Every checkmate is a check, but not every check is a checkmate.

In Diagram 39 White's Queen is checking the Black King. Black has three choices:

He can capture the White Queen with his Rook. He is then no longer in check. See Diagram 40.

He can move his King off the line of attack. He is then no longer in check. See Diagram 41.

Finally, he can interpose one of his men on the line of attack between the White Queen and the King. See Diagram 42. He is then no longer in check.

Diagram 39
BLACK *to move*

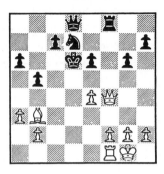

WHITE

Black is in check

Diagram 40
BLACK

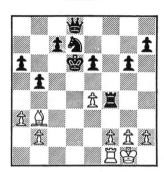

WHITE

Black has captured the
White Queen

Diagram 41
BLACK

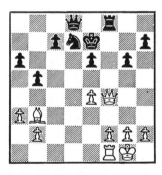

WHITE

Black has moved his King
out of check

Diagram 42
BLACK

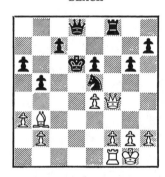

WHITE

Black has interposed his
Knight to get his King out
out of check

But suppose none of these three methods is available? The
King is in check and cannot get out of check. In that case the
King is checkmated, and the game is over.

Diagram 43
BLACK *to move*

WHITE
Black is checkmated

Diagram 44
BLACK

WHITE *to move*
White is checkmated

In Diagram 43 Black's King is checked by a Rook. To move the King sideways does Black no good, as the King will still be in check. But to play the King to his second rank will not do either, since all these squares are controlled by the White Queen, and, as you have learned, a King can never move inside the capturing range of a hostile chessman.

In the position shown in Diagram 44 Black's Queen is checking White's King. The King cannot capture the Queen, as this would bring the King inside the capturing range of the Black Bishop. Interposition is impossible. King moves will not do, as they leave the White King inside the capturing range of Black's Queen. So White is checkmated; Black wins.

To repeat: a King can never move into check—that is, move inside the capturing range of any enemy chessman.

Discovered Check

Most checks come about when a chessman is moved onto a square from which it gives check. However, a discovered ("uncovered") check comes about when a player moves one of his pieces off a line and, thus, opens up a check by one of his other men which has not been moved. An example of this may be found in Diagram

45 where any move by Black's Rook will open up a discovered check by Black's Queen on the diagonal. See Diagram 46.

Diagram 45
BLACK *to move*

WHITE

Black can give a discovered check by moving his Rook

Diagram 46
BLACK

WHITE *to move*

Black has moved his Rook, giving discovered check

Diagram 47
BLACK

WHITE *to move*

White can give a double check by moving his Bishop to the right square

Diagram 48
BLACK *to move*

WHITE

White is giving a double check after having moved his Bishop to the right square

A special form of discovered check is shown as double check. In this case the chessman moving off the line also gives check.

In the case of the simple discovered check, the attacked King can be extricated from the check in any one of three standard methods: capturing the checking piece, moving the King, or interposing.

Where we are dealing with a double check, however, there is only one way out for the attacked King—he must move. To interpose against one check would still leave the King in check; to capture one of the attacking chessmen would still leave the King in check. Diagrams 47 and 48 illustrate a double check.

DRAWN GAMES

So far it may have seemed to the reader that all games must end decisively in victory for White or Black. Actually a game may wind up with honors even, with neither player winning. Such a game is known as a "draw." There are various ways in which such a result may come about.

Draw by Agreement

The players can agree on a draw. This may happen for various reasons: because neither side is able to force checkmate, because there is not enough time to finish the game, because the position is uninteresting, etc.

Draw by Perpetual Check

As the term implies, this refers to a position in which a player can keep checking indefinitely with no possibility of the other player's escaping from the series of checks.

Diagram 49 illustrates such a position. White plays his Queen one square horizontally to the right and gives check. The only way for Black's King to get out of check is to move one square horizontally. See Diagram 50.

Now White moves his Queen one square horizontally and gives

check again. Black moves his King one square horizontally, and we have the position shown in Diagram 49. Obviously White can continue checking indefinitely in this manner. The result is a draw by perpetual check.

The assumption in all cases of perpetual check is that the player who is giving the checks is at a disadvantage and, therefore, chooses to force a draw in order to stave off defeat.

Diagram 49
BLACK

WHITE *to move*
White has a perpetual check

Diagram 50
BLACK

WHITE *to move*
Black cannot escape from the checks

Draw by Insufficient Checkmating Material

As you will see a little later on, there are certain basic, highly simplified positions in which checkmate can be forced against a lone King. King and Queen, for example, or King and Rook can force checkmate against a lone King. However, pieces of lesser power cannot force checkmate in similar circumstances. These include:

> King and Bishop against King
> King and Knight against King
> King and two Knights against King

Draw by Stalemate

Checkmate, we have seen, is a position in which a King is in check and has left only moves that will bring him inside the capturing range of an enemy chessman. The player who has engineered the checkmate is the winner.

Stalemate, however, is a situation in which the player whose turn it is to move is NOT in check but is left without any legal moves.

In Diagram 51 it is White's turn to move. His King is *not* in check. However, any move that White can make would put his King inside the capturing range of Black's Queen. Therefore, White is stalemated, and the game is a draw.

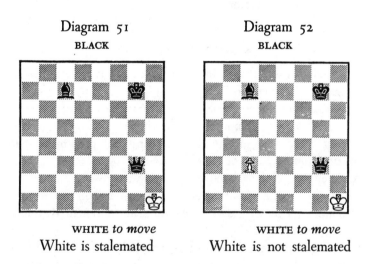

Diagram 51
BLACK

WHITE *to move*
White is stalemated

Diagram 52
BLACK

WHITE *to move*
White is not stalemated

(Note, however, that if it were *Black's* turn to move, he would give checkmate at once in the manner of Diagram 44.)

In Diagram 52, however, the situation is different. White's legal moves are not exhausted because he can still *move his Pawn.* Hence, he is not stalemated and the game is not a draw. In fact, after the Pawn moves, Black forces mate (checkmate) in the manner shown in Diagram 44.

Draw by Repetition of Moves

If the same position is about to occur for the third time with the same player about to move each time, he may claim a draw before actually making the move that produces the threefold repetition.

Draw by Fifty-Move Rule

If a player can demonstrate that the last 50 moves have been made without the capture of a piece or a move by a Pawn, he has the right to claim a draw. To demonstrate such a draw, it would be necessary to keep a record of the game. How this is done will be shown in the next chapter.

LEGAL AND ILLEGAL MOVES

A legal move is one that is in accord with the rules of chess as explained in this chapter.

An illegal move is one that violates these rules.

Examples of illegal moves are: moving the King inside the capturing range of an enemy chessman and making a move that opens up an enemy line of attack on one's King.

Another type of illegal move is one which involves moving a chessman in a manner that differs from its prescribed powers.

Generally speaking, moves or captures are optional. But note these exceptions:

If a King is in check, he must be extricated at once from check. If there is only one way to do it, then that move or capture is compulsory.

A player can never refuse to move. He must always take his turn to move, even if he is limited to disadvantageous moves.

The penalty for an illegal move is that it must be retracted and, if possible, a legal move be made with the same chessman. (Sometimes such a move can be very disadvantageous.) If it is impossible to make a legal move with the same chessman, then no penalty is exacted.

If it is a player's turn to move and he touches one of his pieces or Pawns, he must, if it is legally possible, move the man he touched. If, however, he merely wishes to adjust one of the men, he must say something like "I adjust" or *"J'adoube."*

If it is a player's turn to move and he touches one of his opponent's chessmen, he must try to capture it. Since any of these penalties may prove quite burdensome if not downright fatal, one should be extremely careful in making moves or even touching any chessman.

FOURTH REVIEW TEST
(answers on page 39)

1. When the King is attacked and cannot escape from attack, he is said to be _____.
2. Any attack on the King is called a _____.
3. There are _____ (number) ways to get out of check.
4. One way to get out of check is to _____ the hostile chessman that is giving check.
5. Another way to get out of check is to move the attacked _____ off the line of attack.
6. Still another way of getting out of check is to _____ between the King and the hostile man that is giving check.
7. If none of these ways of getting out of check is available, the King is _____.
8. Every checkmate is a _____, but not every _____ is a checkmate.
9. A _____ can never move into the capturing range of an enemy chessman.
10. [Diagram 43] Black's King (can/cannot) move to his second rank. Reason?
11. [Diagram 44] White's King (can/cannot) capture the Black Queen. Reason?
12. A _____ check comes about when a player moves one of his pieces off a line and thus opens up a check by one of his other men that has not been moved .

13. Double check is a special form of _____ check.
14. The only way to get out of a double check is to move the _____.
15. A _____ occurs when the game winds up with neither player winning.
16. When a player can keep checking indefinitely with no possibility of his opponent's escaping from the series of checks, the game is drawn by _____ _____.
17. King and Queen (can/cannot) force checkmate against a lone King.
18. King and Rook (can/cannot) force checkmate against a lone King.
19. King and Bishop (can/cannot) force checkmate against a lone King.
20. King and two Knights against lone King is a (win/draw).
21. When a player's King is not in check, but it is his turn to move and he has no legal moves left, his King is _____ and the game is a _____.
22. [Diagram 51] White's King (has/does not have) a legal move.
23. If it is Black's turn to move in Diagram 51, what is the result?
24. If a position is about to occur for the third time with the same player about to move each time, he may claim a _____ before actually making the move that produces the threefold repetition.
25. If 50 moves have taken place and no Pawn has been moved and no piece captured, either player may claim a _____.
26. Making a move that opens up an enemy line of attack on one's King is _____.
27. If there is only one way to get a King out of check, then that move is _____.
28. A player (can/cannot) pass up his turn to move.

Fourth Review Test: Answers

1. checkmated
2. check
3. three
4. capture
5. King
6. interpose
7. checkmated
8. check; check
9. King
10. cannot; the King cannot move to the second rank as this would place the King inside the capturing range of White's Queen
11. cannot; the capture would place White's King inside the capturing range of of the Black Bishop
12. discovered
13. discovered
14. King
15. draw
16. perpetual check
17. can
18. can
19. cannot
20. draw
21. stalemated; draw
22. does not
23. Black checkmates in the manner of Diagram 44
24. draw
25. draw
26. illegal
27. compulsory
28. cannot

CHAPTER 2

CHESS NOTATION
AND RELATIVE VALUES

ALL THE material in the previous chapter contains facts that you *must* know in order to play chess, good or bad.

The material in this chapter is optional reading. But it is extremely important in helping you to become a better player and to get more enjoyment out of the game.

CHESS NOTATION

In order to keep a record of a game for future reference, it is necessary to be able to describe a move in a way that will be universally understood. With such a record we can examine our own games or those of others, we can analyze the play, and we can derive enjoyment and instruction from the moves that were played as well as those that might have been played. In looking back over a game, we can learn something from the good moves and perhaps even more from the mistakes.

There are several systems of notation. We shall confine ourselves to the "descriptive notation" used almost exclusively in the United States and Great Britain.

The system is based on the following requirements. Each chessman and each square on the board must have a definite name. Each move will then be recorded as the movement of a specific chessman from one named square to another named square or as the capture of a specific chessman by another man on the opposing side. For the sake of convenience and speed it is customary to use abbreviations. In order to establish the exact sequence of the moves, they are numbered at the left.

In Diagram 2 starting from the left the abbreviations for the chessmen are:

Queen Rook	QR
Queen Knight	QN
Queen Bishop	QB
Queen	Q
King	K
King Bishop	KB
King Knight	KN
King Rook	KR

Where there is no need to specify "Queen Rook" or "King Rook," for example, we simply write R for Rook, N for Knight, and B for Bishop.

Again referring to Diagram 2, we note that the Pawns are named for the pieces in front of which they are placed. Reading from left to right, we get:

Queen Rook Pawn	QRP
Queen Knight Pawn	QNP
Queen Bishop Pawn	QBP
Queen Pawn	QP
King Pawn	KP
King Bishop Pawn	KBP
King Knight Pawn	KNP
King Rook Pawn	KRP

As a rule it is not necessary to specify which Pawn has moved, and it is sufficient to write P for Pawn.

The name of each square is based on the file and rank in which it is located. We number the ranks 1 to 8 from each side of the board. When writing White's moves, we number the ranks and squares from his side of the board. When writing Black's moves, we number the ranks and squares from his side of the board.

As we learned earlier, the files are named for the pieces that stand on them at the beginning of the game. Thus, the file on which the Kings stand at the beginning of the game is called the "King file."

The square on which White's King stands at the beginning of the game (Diagram 2) is called "King 1" or "K1"—a combination of King file and first rank. The square on which the White King Pawn stands at the beginning of the game is called "King 2" or "K2."

Note that while these squares are called K1 and K2 for White's moves, they are called K8 and K7, respectively, for Black's moves. The double name for each square is shown in Diagram 53.

Diagram 53

BLACK

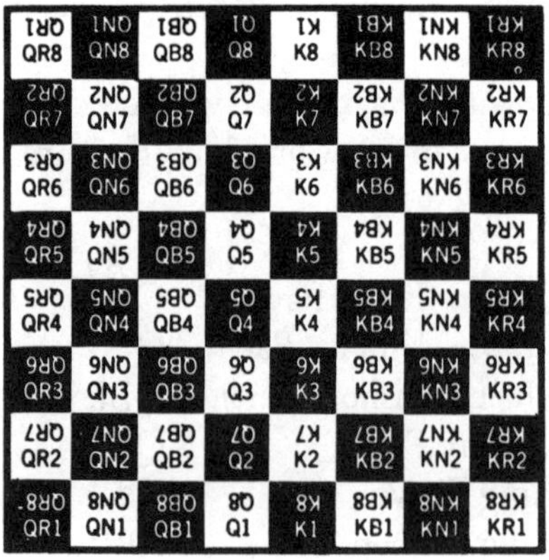

Each square shows two names: the upper (inverted) name is Black's, the lower name is White's.

QR1 / QR8	QN1 / QN8	QB1 / QB8	Q1 / Q8	K1 / K8	KB1 / KB8	KN1 / KN8	KR1 / KR8
QR2 / QR7	QN2 / QN7	QB2 / QB7	Q2 / Q7	K2 / K7	KB2 / KB7	KN2 / KN7	KR2 / KR7
QR3 / QR6	QN3 / QN6	QB3 / QB6	Q3 / Q6	K3 / K6	KB3 / KB6	KN3 / KN6	KR3 / KR6
QR4 / QR5	QN4 / QN5	QB4 / QB5	Q4 / Q5	K4 / K5	KB4 / KB5	KN4 / KN5	KR4 / KR5
QR5 / QR4	QN5 / QN4	QB5 / QB4	Q5 / Q4	K5 / K4	KB5 / KB4	KN5 / KN4	KR5 / KR4
QR6 / QR3	QN6 / QN3	QB6 / QB3	Q6 / Q3	K6 / K3	KB6 / KB3	KN6 / KN3	KR6 / KR3
QR7 / QR2	QN7 / QN2	QB7 / QB2	Q7 / Q2	K7 / K2	KB7 / KB2	KN7 / KN2	KR7 / KR2
QR8 / QR1	QN8 / QN1	QB8 / QB1	Q8 / Q1	K8 / K1	KB8 / KB1	KN8 / KN1	KR8 / KR1

WHITE

The names of the squares

The moves are arranged in two columns, one for White's moves and the other for Black's. If White advances his King Pawn two squares, we write 1 P-K4 in White's column. If Black thereupon

advances his King Pawn two squares, we write that move as P-K4.
Here are some of the other symbols used in chess notation:

captures	x
moves to	-
check	ch
discovered check	dis ch
double check	dbl ch
en passant (in passing)	e.p.
a good move	!
a bad move	?
from or at	/
promotes to a Queen	/Q

A few words about these symbols:

If a Queen captures a Bishop, we write QxB.

If a Rook moves to King 8 giving check, we write R-K8 ch.

If we want to indicate that R-K8 ch is a good move, we write
R-K8 ch!

If two Knights are capable of moving to the same square, we
specify in this manner: N/Q3-K5. This means that the Knight
situated at Queen 3 plays to King 5.

If a Pawn moves to King Rook 8 and becomes a Queen, we
write P-R8/Q.

At this point we shall try to play over two brief games in order
to have some practice with chess notation.

Game 1
KING'S GAMBIT DECLINED
(in effect)

	WHITE	BLACK
1	P-K4	P-K4
2	N-QB3	N-QB3
3	P-B4	P-Q3
4	N-B3	P-QR3

See Diagram 54 to check the position.

5	B-B4	B-N5
6	PxP	NxP
7	NxN!	BxQ
8	BxPch	K-K2
9	N-Q5 mate	

See Diagram 55 to check the final position.

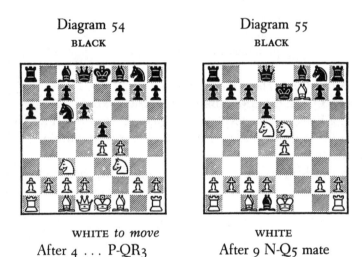

Diagram 54	Diagram 55
BLACK	BLACK
WHITE *to move*	WHITE
After 4 ... P-QR3	After 9 N-Q5 mate

Here is another short game given to provide more practice in using chess notation.

Game 2
SICILIAN DEFENSE

WHITE		BLACK
1	P-K4	P-QB4
2	N-KB3	P-Q3
3	N-B3	P-K4
4	B-B4	N-QB3

| 5 | P-Q3 | KN-K2 |

See Diagram 56 to check the position.

6	B-KN5	B-N5
7	N-Q5	N-Q5
8	NxP!	BxQ
9	N-KB6ch!	NPxN
10	BxP mate	

See Diagram 57 to check the final position.

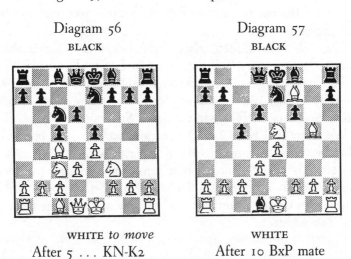

Diagram 56	Diagram 57
BLACK	BLACK
WHITE *to move*	WHITE
After 5 ... KN-K2	After 10 BxP mate

RELATIVE VALUES OF THE CHESSMEN

It is of the greatest importance to have a clear and reliable notion of the value of each chessman. (We omit the King from this calculation because his value is absolute.)

The following table gives this information. It is based partly on the mobility of each chessman, reinforced by the experience of centuries.

Queen   9

Rook	5
Bishop	3
Knight	3
Pawn	1

What does the table tell us?

Suppose you can capture a Bishop while letting your opponent capture your Knight. There is no harm done, as Bishop and Knight have the same value. (Such a pair of captures is called an exchange.)

On the other hand, if you capture a Pawn and your opponent captures a Bishop, you come off badly because you have lost by the exchange.

The table tells us, then, what kinds of captures are profitable, what kinds are costly, and what kinds are neutral.

The reason why we have to weigh captures and exchanges so carefully is this: when a player obtains a net superiority in material, he is very likely to win the game. *Superior force wins.*

We know that King and Queen can checkmate the opposing King by force. This means that if a player wins his opponent's Queen early in the game, he is sure to win. As a matter of fact, if he wins only a Pawn he is likely to win the game, because the extra Pawn can be escorted to the last row and converted into a brand-new Queen.

A Rook is worth more than a Bishop or Knight. (This is known as having the advantage of the "Exchange.") A Rook is worth more than a Bishop or Knight plus a Pawn. However, a Bishop (or Knight) plus two Pawns should generally win against a Rook.

Also, Bishop and Knight almost always win against Rook and Pawn. However, Bishop and Knight against Rook and two Pawns results in a toss-up with the odds favoring the Rook.

Superior force wins. So strongly ingrained is this concept that most players when they are hopelessly down in material will "resign" the game instead of waiting helplessly to be checkmated. Resigning, then, is simply conceding defeat without the agony of waiting to be checkmated.

There are times, to be sure, when a player is amply justified in giving up material. He may have in mind a crafty sequence whereby he gains an immediate and overwhelming repayment of the material so invested. Strangely enough the purposeful loss of material is called a "sacrifice," though in the interests of accuracy it should be called an "investment."

Consider, for example, the play in Game 1 (page 43), where White sacrifices his Queen with 7 NxN! because he foresees that he will force checkmate two moves later. Game 2 (page 44) has a very similar sequence. Here, too, White sacrifices his Queen—and then a Knight as well—in order to force an immediate mate.

Generally speaking, though, loss of material is due to sheer incompetence and the resulting loss of the game is a well deserved punishment.

We leave the problems of winning or losing material to a later chapter. This is a good place, however, to give some examples of even exchanges from practical play.

In Diagram 58 White is threatening to win a piece by PxB. Black plays . . . BxN and White replies QxB. The players remain even in material.

In Diagram 59 Black is threatening to win a Pawn by . . . PxP. White plays PxP and Black replies . . . QxP. The players are still even in material.

Diagram 58	Diagram 59
BLACK *to move*	BLACK

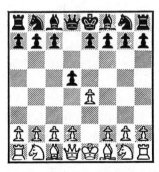

WHITE	WHITE *to move*
After P-KR3	After . . . P-Q4

FIFTH REVIEW TEST
(answers on pages 50–51)

1. Chess notation requires a specific name for each _____ and for each _____.
2. The abbreviation for Queen Rook is _____.
3. The abbreviation for King Knight is _____.
4. K is the abbreviation for _____.
5. _____ are named for the pieces in front of which they are located at the beginning of the game.
6. Horizontal rows of squares are called _____.
7. Vertical rows of squares are called _____.
8. The name of a square is determined by its _____ and _____.
9. The abbreviation for Queen Bishop Pawn is _____.
10. We number the _____ 1 to 8 from each side of the board.
11. When writing White's moves, we number the ranks and squares from _____ side of the board.
12. The _____ are named for the pieces that stand on them at the beginning of the game.
13. The file on which the Queens stand at the beginning of the game is called the _____ file.
14. The square on which the White King Rook stands at the beginning of the game is called _____ _____ from White's side of the board and _____ _____ from Black's side of the board.
15. The square called King 5 (K5) from White's side of the board is called _____( ) from Black's side of the board.
16. The square called Queen Bishop 6 (QB6) from Black's side of the board is called _____( ) from White's side of the board.
17. The square called Queen Rook 7 (QR7) from White's side of the board is called [QueenRook 7 (QR7)/Queen Rook 2 (QR2)] from Black's side of the board.
18. The square called Queen 4 (Q4) from Black's side of the

board (is/is not) called Queen 4 (Q4) from White's side.

19. If White starts the game by advancing his Queen Pawn two squares, we write the move as _____.

20. If Black replies by advancing his King Bishop Pawn two squares, we write that move as _____.

21. The symbol for a bad move is _____.

22. e.p. is the symbol for _____ _____.

23. ! is the symbol for a _____ move.

24. The symbol for check is _____.

25. The symbol for captures is _____.

26. The symbol for "moves to" is _____.

27. If R-K5 is a discovered check, we write the move as_____ _____ _____.

28. If Q-K3 is a bad move, we write the move as _____ _____.

29. If it is necessary to show that the move R-B7 was made by a Rook starting from Q7, we write the move as _____.

30. If a Pawn moves from King 7 to King 8, we write the move as _____.

31. In Game 1 we (can/cannot) write White's second move as 2 N-B3. Reason?

32. In Game 1 White's fifth move (should/should not) be written as 5 B-QB4. Reason?

33. In Game 1 White's sixth move (should/should not) be written as 5 QPxKP. Reason?

34. In Game 2 White's third move (should/should not) be written as 3 N-QB3. Reason?

35. In Game 2 Black's fifth move (should/should not) be written as 5 ... N-K2.

36. In the table of relative values the Queen is valued at _____(number) points.

37. A Bishop and Knight (are/are not) of the same value.

38. In Game 2 Black (can/cannot) play 10 ... KxB or 10 ... K-Q2. Reason?

39. It (is/is not) advantageous to give up a Bishop in return for a Pawn. Reason?

40. A King and Queen (can/cannot) force checkmate against the opposing King.

41. King and Pawn can achieve the same result through Pawn _____.

42. When a player is hopelessly behind in material, he often concedes defeat by _____.

43. A move that gives up material in the hope of superior compensation is called a _____.

Fifth Review Test: Answers

1. chessman; square
2. QR
3. KN
4. King
5. Pawns
6. ranks
7. files
8. file; rank
9. QBP
10. ranks
11. White's
12. files
13. Queen
14. King Rook 1 (KR1); King Rook 8 (KR8)
15. King 4 (K4)
16. Queen Bishop 3 (QB3)
17. Queen Rook 2 (QR2)
18. is not
19. P-Q4
20. P-KB4
21. ?
22. *en passant*
23. good
24. ch
25. x

26. -
27. R-K5 dis ch
28. Q-K3?
29. R/Q7-B7
30. P-K8/Q
31. cannot; we would not know whether White played out his King Knight or Queen Knight
32. should not; White's other Bishop cannot move, so there is no need to specify which Bishop 4 is being occupied.
33. should not; only the Queen Pawn can capture, and only the King Pawn can capture; hence, the Pawns do not have to be specified
34. should not; the other White Knight has already been moved, so there can be no doubt as to which Knight is being moved now

35. should not; either Black Knight can go to King 2
36. 9
37. are
38. cannot; either move would bring the Black Knight inside the capturing range of White's Knight

39. is not; a Bishop is much more valuable than a Pawn
40. can
41. promotion
42. resigning
43. sacrifice

CHAPTER 3

THE ART OF CHECKMATE

MOST GAMES end with the resignation of one of the players. Nevertheless, the knowledge of how to force checkmate lies at the very heart of chess. In this chapter we shall deal with the basic checkmates against a lone King, and we shall then go on to some typical checkmating patterns which can occur in the earlier part of a game.

THE BASIC CHECKMATES

We have referred earlier to the basic checkmates that can be forced against a lone King. It is essential to be able to execute these checkmates; without this knowledge it may become impossible, or at any rate embarrassingly difficult, to bring a winning game to an appropriate conclusion.

Checkmate with the Queen

Since the Queen is the most powerful piece, it follows that this will be the easiest of the basic checkmates to enforce. Such a checkmate involves the following:

(a) The hostile King must be driven to one of the sides of the board.

(b) To accomplish this, the Queen cuts off the King's mobility —that is, drives him away from the center of the board.

(c) The Queen is assisted in this task by her King.

(d) The Queen's powers of moving vertically, horizontally, and diagonally play an important role.

Diagrams 60 and 61 illustrate typical checkmating situations with the Queen. In each case you will note that the weaker side's King is in check and is left only with moves that would bring him inside the capturing range of the hostile pieces.

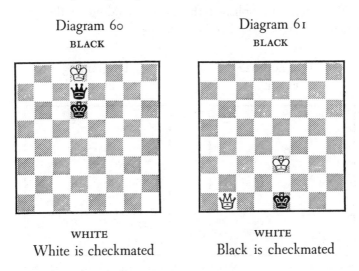

Diagram 60	Diagram 61
BLACK	BLACK
WHITE	WHITE
White is checkmated	Black is checkmated

In Diagram 62 White begins by restricting the mobility of Black's King:

WHITE	BLACK
1 Q-N5!	K-K3

Now Black's King is confined to three ranks, and White's King can come in for the kill.

2	K-N2	K-Q3
3	K-B3	K-K3
4	K-Q4	K-Q3

5	Q-N6ch	K-K2

Black's King is being forced to the side of the board.

6	K-K5	K-Q2
7	Q-N7ch	K-K1
8	K-B6	K-B1
9	Q-KB7 mate	

White has accomplished the mate according to the pattern shown in Diagram 60. See Diagram 63.

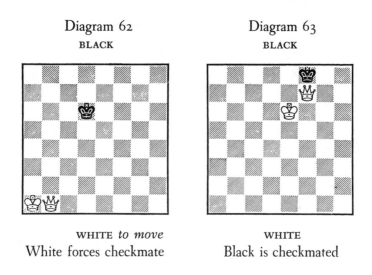

Diagram 62
BLACK

Diagram 63
BLACK

WHITE *to move*
White forces checkmate

WHITE
Black is checkmated

Checkmate with the Rook

This mate is somewhat lengthier, as the Rook lacks the diagonal powers of the Queen. However, it is not too difficult to achieve the mate if one applies the restrictive technique. Follow the play from Diagram 64:

	WHITE	BLACK
1	R-K1!	. . . .

This cuts the Black King off from a considerable portion of the board.

1	....	K-Q5
2	K-N2	K-Q6
3	R-K8	K-Q5
4	K-B2	K-Q4
5	K-B3	K-B4
6	R-Q8!	....

Forcing the Black King toward the side of the board.

6	....	K-B3
7	K-B4	K-B2
8	R-Q1	K-B3
9	R-Q2	K-N3
10	R-Q6ch	K-B2
11	K-B5	....

White is aiming for the mating pattern of Diagram 61.

11	....	K-N2
12	R-Q7ch	K-B1

Diagram 64	Diagram 65
BLACK	BLACK

WHITE	WHITE
White forces checkmate	Black is checkmated

13	K-B6	K-N1
14	R-Q8ch	K-R2
15	R-KR8	K-R3
16	R-R8 mate	

Compare Diagrams 61 and 65.

Checkmate with the Two Bishops

A single Bishop, as we know, cannot force checkmate. However, the two Bishops, assisted by their King, can do the trick. Diagram 67 shows the desired mating position. Note that in addition to driving the King to the side, the winning player can force the mate only when the hostile King is on a corner square.

The play starts from Diagram 66:

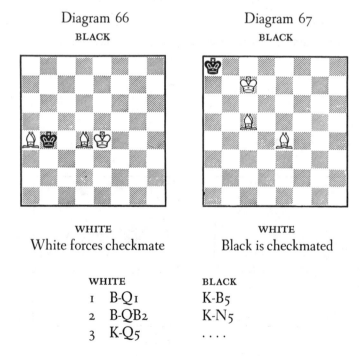

Diagram 66	Diagram 67
BLACK	BLACK
WHITE	WHITE
White forces checkmate	Black is checkmated

WHITE		BLACK
1	B-Q1	K-B5
2	B-QB2	K-N5
3	K-Q5	. . . .

White begins the process of forcing back the Black King.

3	. . . .	K-N4
4	B-QB5	K-R3
5	K-B6	K-R4
6	B-Q6	K-R3

The Black King has been forced to the side of the board.

7	B-N4	K-R2
8	K-B7	K-R3
9	B-Q3ch	K-R2
10	B-B5ch	K-R1
11	B-K4 mate	

See Diagram 67.

Checkmate with Bishop and Knight

This is the most laborious of the standard checkmates. It is also the most instructive one, for it illustrates the cooperation of the checkmating forces in a most impressive manner.

Note that the King to be checkmated must be forced into a corner square of the same color as those on which the Bishop travels. Consequently, in Diagram 68 the Black King will submit to checkmate on a white corner square.

From Diagram 68 play proceeds as follows:

WHITE		BLACK
1	N-B5	K-Q1
2	N-N7ch	K-B1

The ending, which has started here at rather an advanced stage, requires that Black's King be driven to his Queen Rook 1 square.

3	K-B6	K-N1
4	K-N6	K-B1
5	B-N4ch	K-N1

Diagram 68
BLACK

WHITE *to move*
White forces checkmate

Diagram 69
BLACK

WHITE
Black is checkmated

Black's King is being forced inexorably into the corner.

6	B-B5	K-R1
7	N-B5	K-N1
8	N-R6ch	K-R1
9	B-K4 mate	

The mating position is shown in Diagram 69.

TYPICAL CHECKMATING POSITIONS

So much for the basic checkmating techniques. It is important, however, to be familiar with other patterns that recur frequently and offer the possibility of effecting a quick mate.

Many checkmates are preceded by a sacrifice, which, as we have seen earlier, is an intentional surrender of material for the purpose of securing a greater gain, such as achieving checkmate.

The sequence of moves entailed by a sacrifice is called a "combination." We might define a combination as a series of coordinated moves directed to the attainment of a specific objective.

Double Checks

Since double checks are always vicious and sometimes irresistible, they frequently lead to checkmate. In Diagrams 70 and 71 we

Diagram 70

BLACK

WHITE *to move*

WHITE	BLACK
1 BxQP mate	

Diagram 71

BLACK

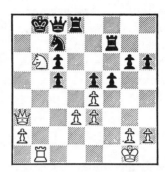

WHITE *to move*

WHITE	BLACK
1 N-Q7 mate	

Diagram 72

BLACK

WHITE *to move*

WHITE	BLACK
1 NxP mate	

Diagram 73

BLACK

WHITE *to move*

WHITE	BLACK
1 B-QN5 mate	

need merely look for an open file and seek an opportunity to make use of it. Diagram 70 calls for action on the King Bishop file, while Diagram 71 presents opportunities on the Queen Knight file.

Actually, if you examine these situations, you will observe that it is not enough to look for an open file; you must look for an open line that is occupied by a King and a hostile Rook or Queen. Try this technique in Diagrams 72 and 73. In the former, White's Queen and Black's King are situated on the same rank. In the latter, Black's King and White's Rook are on the same line.

Note, by the way, that in Diagrams 72-73 Black's King came a cropper because he was badly exposed to attack. The King has no business being located in the crossfire of the enemy pieces.

The Last Rank

Checkmates on the last rank by a Rook or Queen are also of common occurrence. If a player's first rank is not guarded by a Rook, it is often useful to create a "loophole" or escape hatch for his King. Diagrams 74 and 75 show why this is so.

Diagram 74
BLACK

WHITE *to move*

WHITE	BLACK
1 R-Q8ch	RxR
2 RxR mate	

Diagram 75
BLACK

WHITE *to move*

WHITE	BLACK
1 Q-K8ch!	NxQ
2 R-B8 mate	

In Diagram 74 the mate is obvious and direct. In Diagram 75 it is well concealed; here we need a spectacular Queen sacrifice to create a mating position.

Diagrams 74 and 75 have one feature in common that should give us pause. In both cases Black is ahead in material, and yet he loses in jig time. What then happens to our rule that superior force wins? We must modify it by saying that superior force wins except in those cases where the *positional* advantage lies with the player who is behind in material.

In Diagrams 76 and 77 a neat Queen sacrifice is the prelude to the checkmate. Note a further characteristic feature: the loser's Queen is out of play. You will often find this true of situations where a player can successfully sacrifice his Queen. It stands to reason that a player will find himself vulnerable when his Queen has nothing to contribute to the defense.

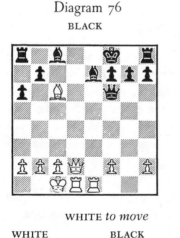

Diagram 76	Diagram 77
BLACK	BLACK *to move*
WHITE *to move*	WHITE

WHITE	BLACK	WHITE	BLACK
1 Q-Q8ch!	BxQ	1	QxRch!
2 R-K8 mate		2 KxQ	R-B8 mate

Note the similarity between the mates in Diagrams 75 and 77.

In Diagrams 78 and 79 we again see Queen sacrifices directed against uncastled Kings. Repeatedly we find that a King placed in the crossfire of the opposing pieces is in serious danger.

Diagram 78
BLACK

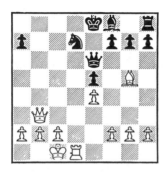

WHITE *to move*

WHITE	BLACK
1 Q-N8ch!	NxQ
2 R-Q8 mate	

Diagram 79
BLACK

WHITE *to move*

WHITE	BLACK
1 Q-B8ch!	RxQ
2 RxR mate	

King in the Center

We have already given several examples of successful attack against a King stranded in the center. It is on this part of the board that the other pieces are at their most effective, as they can switch rapidly to any other part of the board. By the same token, this is the most dangerous area for the King. All these examples drive home the same lesson: the King must be moved early in the game into a safe position.

In Diagrams 82 and 83 the Black King again runs into trouble —in the second case a Queen sacrifice was necessary, while in the first no sacrifice was needed. The moral is clear: *Safeguard your King.*

Open Files

An open file leading into the heart of the enemy camp will often spell disaster for the defender, especially if the attacker occupies the open line in force. In Diagram 84 Black has all three "heavy" pieces on the open Queen Knight file. White's protecting phalanx

Diagram 80

BLACK

WHITE *to move*

WHITE	BLACK
1 B-B4 mate	

Diagram 81

BLACK

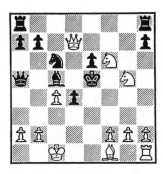

WHITE *to move*

WHITE	BLACK
1 QxKPch	K-B5
2 N-R3 mate	

Diagram 82

BLACK

WHITE *to move*

WHITE	BLACK
1 P-B5ch	K-K3
2 Q-N3 mate	

Diagram 83

BLACK

WHITE *to move*

WHITE	BLACK
1 Q-Q5ch!	NxQ
2 PxN mate	

of Pawns has been stripped away and his Queen is removed from the scene of action. The quick finish does not, therefore, come as a great surprise.

In Diagram 85 Black's command of the open King Knight file leads to an even more remarkable finish.

Diagram 84	Diagram 85
BLACK *to move*	BLACK *to move*

WHITE		WHITE	
WHITE	BLACK	WHITE	BLACK
1	R-R6ch!	1	Q-N6ch!
2 RxR	Q-N7 mate	2 PxQ	PxP mate

Not only is White's Queen useless in Diagram 85, but she even blocks the White King's escape from the mate.

In Diagram 86 White is a piece down, so he must seek substantial compensation. He finds it in his occupation of the King Rook file. This enables him to penetrate decisively into the Black King's castled position.

In Diagram 87, too, the open King Rook file is White's highway to victory. The plausible 1 Q-R7ch leads to nothing after 1 . . . K-B1. So White needs something stronger if he is to overcome his deficiency in material. He finds it in 1 R-R8ch! nailing down Black's King for the coming checkmate.

Note an interesting point about Diagram 87. Black cannot play 1 . . . BxR, as this would expose his King to attack. We say that the Bishop is "pinned" by White's Queen—a pinned piece being one which screens a more valuable piece from attack. As we shall see later on, a pinned piece, because of its sinister immobility, can be dangerously vulnerable to attack.

Diagram 86

BLACK

WHITE *to move*

WHITE	BLACK
1 R-KN7ch!	KxR
2 Q-R7 mate	

Diagram 87

BLACK

WHITE *to move*

WHITE	BLACK
1 R-R8ch!	KxR
2 Q-R7 mate	

The Seventh Rank

Attacks on the seventh rank, either by two Rooks or by the Queen acting in concert with a Rook, can be very powerful. Pieces posted on this rank are in the very heart of enemy territory; hence, it is not surprising that they wreak such havoc.

In Diagram 88 White is threatening checkmate. But it is Black's turn to move, and he is the one who forces checkmate.

In Diagram 89 Black's checkmating method is exceedingly artistic.

In Diagram 90 White's pieces offer no support whatever to their menaced King. This is strikingly true of the White Queen.

In Diagram 91 this is also true of White's pieces. In fact, they actually block the escape of White's King!

In both cases the cooperation of the Black pieces is beautiful.

Rook and Knight Patterns

The powers of the Rook and the Knight are so different that, when they act in concert, they make a powerful team.

Diagram 88
BLACK *to move*

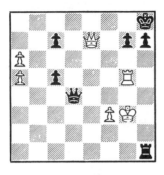

WHITE

WHITE	BLACK
1	Q-KR5ch
2 K-N2	Q-R7 mate

Diagram 89
BLACK *to move*

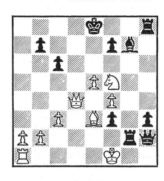

WHITE

WHITE	BLACK
1	R-N8ch!
2 BxR	Q-K7 mate

Diagram 90
BLACK *to move*

WHITE

WHITE	BLACK
1	R-B7ch
2 K-Q1	N-K6 mate

Diagram 91
BLACK *to move*

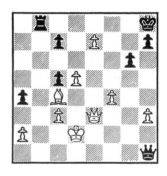

WHITE

WHITE	BLACK
1	R-N7ch
2 K-Q3	Q-QN8 mate

Diagram 92 shows a typical pattern which has many practical applications.

The pattern shown in Diagram 93 is somewhat less common but none the less effective.

Diagram 92
BLACK *to move*

WHITE

WHITE	BLACK
1	QxRPch!
2 RxQ	R-N8 mate

Diagram 93
BLACK

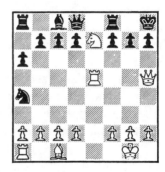

WHITE *to move*

WHITE	BLACK
1 QxRPch!	KxQ
2 R-KR5 mate	

Diagram 94
BLACK *to move*

WHITE

WHITE	BLACK
1	QxRPch!
2 KxQ	R-R4 mate

Diagram 95
BLACK

WHITE *to move*

WHITE	BLACK
1 Q-B6ch	K-N1
2 Q-N7 mate	

Pawn Wedges

We use this term to describe a far advanced Pawn which makes checkmate possible. The patterns are typical and opportunities to employ them are quite frequent.

In Diagram 94 Black's Pawn wedge cuts off the White King's flight to King Knight 2.

In Diagram 95 White delivers checkmate on King Knight 7 with his Queen.

Diagram 96 is an elaborate version of Diagram 94. In both cases the Pawn wedge prevents the flight of the hostile King.

In Diagram 97 we see how a Pawn wedge at King Knight 6 makes it possible to mate with the Queen at King Rook 7.

The Long Diagonal

The long diagonal reaches from corner to corner. When a Bishop is posted on this diagonal he can menace the hostile King from quite a distance.

In Diagram 98, for example, White's well timed Pawn check opens up the long diagonal in devastating fashion.

And in Diagram 99 we find that Black's Bishop functions powerfully from Queen Knight 2, even though the long diagonal appears at first to be blocked.

The Two Bishops

Two Bishops cooperating on powerful diagonals make up one of the most formidable forces that can be assembled on the chessboard. Woe to any King who finds himself in their crossfire!

In Diagram 100 the White Bishops command two magnificent diagonals, a position which causes disaster for the Black King.

In Diagram 101 we see a typical mating pattern with the two Bishops.

In Diagram 102 we have a more elaborate example of the pattern of Diagram 100, and there is a similar relationship between Diagram 101 and Diagram 103.

Diagram 96

BLACK

WHITE *to move*

WHITE	BLACK
1 QxRPch!	KxQ
2 R-R4ch	Q-R3
3 RxQ mate	

Diagram 97

BLACK *to move*

WHITE

WHITE	BLACK
1	RxPch!
2 PxR	Q-R7 mate

Diagram 98

BLACK

WHITE *to move*

WHITE	BLACK
1 P-B7ch	RxP
2 R-R8 mate	

Diagram 99

BLACK *to move*

WHITE

WHITE	BLACK
1	RxPch!
2 BxR	QxB mate

Diagram 100

BLACK

WHITE *to move*

WHITE	BLACK
1 B-N6 mate	

Diagram 101

BLACK *to move*

WHITE

WHITE	BLACK
1	B-B6 mate

Diagram 102

BLACK

WHITE *to move*

WHITE	BLACK
1 QxPch!	PxQ
2 B-QR6 mate	

Diagram 103

BLACK *to move*

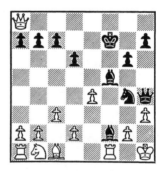

WHITE

WHITE	BLACK
1	QxPch!
2 PxQ	BxP mate

Pins

We had an earlier example of a pin in Diagram 87, which should
be reviewed here.

In Diagram 104 the mate is based on the fact that Black's Rook at King Knight 3 is pinned by White's Rook at King Knight 2 and, therefore, cannot capture White's Queen.

Similarly, in Diagram 105 Black's Queen is pinned by White's Bishop at Queen 6 and again cannot capture White's Queen.

Diagram 104

BLACK

WHITE *to move*

WHITE	BLACK
1 Q-R6 mate	

Diagram 105

BLACK

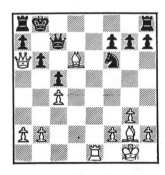

WHITE *to move*

WHITE	BLACK
1 Q-N7 mate	

Diagram 106

BLACK

WHITE *to move*

WHITE	BLACK
1 N-Q6 mate	

Diagram 107

BLACK

WHITE *to move*

WHITE	BLACK
1 QxP mate	

The pin is again operative in Diagram 106, where Black cannot play 1 ... BxN because the Bishop is pinned by White's Rook at King 1, and in Diagram 107, where Black cannot play 1 ... PxQ because his King Knight Pawn is pinned by White's Bishop at King Bishop 5. (Note, by the way, the power of White's united Bishops in this situation.)

In Diagram 108 Black cannot play 3 ... NxR because his Knight at King Bishop 4 is pinned by White's Bishop at Queen Bishop 2.

In Diagram 109 Black cannot interpose 3 R-B1 because his Rook is pinned by Black's Bishop at Queen Bishop 4.

Diagram 108	Diagram 109
BLACK	BLACK *to move*

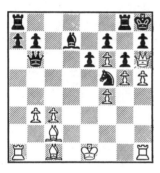

WHITE *to move*	WHITE

WHITE	BLACK	WHITE	BLACK
1 QxRPch!	KxQ	1	QxNch!
2 PxP dbl ch	KxP	2 KxQ	R-Q8 mate
3 R-R6 mate			

SIXTH REVIEW TEST
(*answers on pages 74–75*)

1. The easiest of the basic checkmates is that of King and _____ against a lone King.
2. In the mate involving King and Queen against King, the first

task is to drive the weaker King away from the _____ of the board.

3. This will result in the weaker King's being driven to one of the _____ rows of the board.

4. To execute this task, the Queen needs the help of her _____.

5. The Queen does an effective job because she is able to move vertically, horizontally, and _____.

6. [Diagram 60] If White were to play KxQ that (would be/would not be) an illegal move. Reason?

7. [Diagram 61] Black's King (can/cannot) play to his seventh rank. Reason?

8. In the play starting from Diagram 62, 2 Q-QN6ch (would/would not) be an inferior move. Reason?

9. To checkmate with the Rook is somewhat harder than with the Queen because the Rook cannot move on _____.

10. [Diagram 64] 1 R-Q1ch (would/would not) be a good move. Reason?

11. The basic checkmate of King and two Bishops against a lone King can take place only when the weaker side's King has been driven to a _____ square.

12. The basic checkmate of King, Bishop, and Knight against a lone King (is/is not) the hardest of all the basic checkmates.

13. This checkmate (can/cannot) take place only when the weaker side's King has been forced to a corner square of the right color.

14. Checkmates at an earlier stage of the game are often preceded by a _____.

15. A _____ is a series of coordinated moves directed to the attainment of a specific objective.

16. [Diagram 70] Black cannot play 1 ... PxB or 1 ... BxB because his King would still be in _____.

17. [Diagram 71] White gives a double check with his _____ and _____.

18. [Diagram 72] Black (can/cannot) play 1 ... K-N4. Reason?

19. [Diagram 73] Black (can/cannot) reply 1 ... N-K5 or 1 ... B-K2. Reason?

20. [Diagram 74] If Black's King Rook Pawn were on King Rook 3, the mate (would/would not) be possible. Reason?
21. [Diagram 75] If Black's Knight were on Queen 2, the mate (would/would not) be possible. Reason?
22. [Diagram 76] The mate (would/would not) be possible if Black's King Knight Pawn were at King Knight 3.
23. [Diagram 77] The mate (would/would not) be possible if White's Queen were at King Knight 3. Reason?
24. [Diagram 78] The mate (would/would not) be possible if Black's Bishop were at Queen 3. Reason?
25. [Diagram 79] If Black's Knight were at Queen 2 and White played 1 R-N3, Black's best defense would be 1 ... _____.
26. [Diagram 84] Mate (would still/would not still) be possible if White's Queen were at Queen Bishop 2.
27. [Diagram 87] Black cannot answer 1 R-R8ch with 1 ... BxR because Black's Bishop is _____.
28. [Diagram 89] If White's Bishop were at King Knight 1, Black would win with 1 ... _____; 2 _____, _____ mate.
29. [Diagram 94] Black cannot force mate with 1 ... R-R4 because White has the reply 2 _____.
30. [Diagram 103] Black can also play 1 ... Q-N6. Then after 2 PxN, he continues 2 ... _____ mate.
31. [Diagram 108] White can also win with 1 BxN. If Black replies 1 ... NPxB, White wins with 2 _____, etc. But if Black replies ... KPxB, White wins brilliantly with 2 _____ ch!, _____; 3 _____ dbl ch, _____; 4 _____ mate.

Sixth Review Test: Answers

1. Queen
2. center
3. side
4. King

5. diagonally
6. would be; White's King cannot enter the capturing range of Black's King

7. cannot; Black's King cannot enter the capturing range of White's King
8. would; it would give Black's King too much scope
9. diagonals
10. would not; it would give Black's King too much scope
11. corner
12. is
13. can
14. sacrifice
15. combination
16. check
17. Rook; Knight
18. cannot; the Black King would enter the capturing range of White's Knight
19. cannot; the Black King would still be in check from the White Bishop
20. would not; Black's King could escape via King Rook 2

21. would not; after 2 R-B8ch, Black could reply 2 ... NxR
22. would not; Black's King could escape via King Knight 2
23. would not; after 2 ... R-B8ch, White could reply 3 Q-N1
24. would not; after 1 Q-N8ch, Black could reply 1 ... BxQ or ... NxQ
25. 1 ... QxR/Q8ch
26. would not be
27. pinned
28. 1 ... RxBch; 2 QxR, Q-K7 mate
29. P-KN4
30. Q-R5
31. P-N6; 2 QxRPch!, KxQ; 3 PxP dbl ch, KxP; 4 R-R6 mate

CHAPTER 4

HOW TO WIN MATERIAL

THOUGH THE thought of checkmate must always be uppermost in our minds, it is generally an ultimate goal rather than a direct object.

But what we can strive for much more rapidly, and often with success, is the winning of material. You will recall that we have stressed the important principle that *superior force wins*. Almost invariably when a player is ahead in material, he is able to bend his opponent to his will, either by simplifying the game into one which is easily won or by conducting an attack which, by virtue of his plus material, cannot be parried by his handicapped opponent.

This chapter will deal with some of the chief ways in which material can be won.

DOUBLE ATTACK

This is a simultaneous attack by one chessman on two hostile units. It is often combined with a check or a mate threat—these make it all the more powerful. All the chessmen are capable of this kind of attack, even the lowly Pawn. However, double attacks by the Knight ("Knight forks") will be considered under a separate heading.

Queen Forks

These are the most powerful of all, thanks to the Queen's enormous powers. Besides double attacks along the same rank, file, or diagonal, the Queen can also attack simultaneously on a rank and file, a rank and diagonal, a file and diagonal, or two diagonals.

Powerful as these attacks are, they can sometimes be parried if one of the attacked units moves off to give check or to evolve a threat that is more formidable than the original attack.

In Diagram 110 White sets up a double attack by first sacrificing the Exchange. This wins one of the Rooks.

In Diagram 111, on the other hand, Black at once sets up a double attack on White's Rook and Bishop, winning at least one of these pieces.

Diagram 110	Diagram 111
BLACK	BLACK *to move*

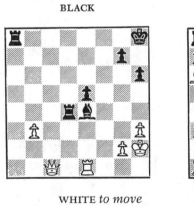

WHITE *to move*		WHITE	
WHITE	BLACK	WHITE	BLACK
1 RxB!	RxR	1	Q-B3 and wins
2 Q-B6 and wins			

Black's procedure in Diagram 111 suggests to us that double attacks are particularly lethal when the targets are unprotected.

This point is repeated in Diagram 112 which shows the White Queen's double attack on Black's unprotected Rook and Knight. This wins a piece.

In Diagram 113 the double attack requires a preparatory move, but the result is the same: two Black pieces are attacked and one of them must fall.

Diagram 112
BLACK

WHITE *to move*

WHITE	BLACK
1 Q-B3 and wins	

Diagram 113
BLACK

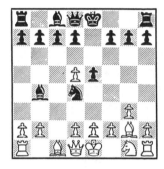

WHITE *to move*

WHITE	BLACK
1 P-K3	N-B4
2 Q-N4 and wins	

Diagram 114
BLACK

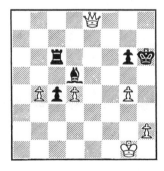

WHITE *to move*

WHITE	BLACK
1 Q-KR8ch	K-N4
2 Q-K5ch and wins	

Diagram 115
BLACK

WHITE *to move*

WHITE	BLACK
1 BxN	QxB
2 Q-Q5ch and wins	

Queen Forks with Checks

These attacks are even stronger than the ones we have just examined, for the attacked King must get out of check.

So in Diagram 114 2 Q-K5ch wins Black's Bishop, while in Diagram 115 White's elimination of the protective Black Knight followed by 2 Q-Q5ch must win a piece. Note here that if Black plays 1 ... QxB or 1 ... PxB, White wins the other Black Knight with 2 Q-Q5ch; but if Black plays 1 ... RxB, then 2 Q-Q5ch wins a Rook.

In Diagram 116 White prepares for 3 Q-Q5ch which wins a Rook. It does not matter whether he begins with 1 NxN or 1 BxN.

In Diagram 117 Black wins only a Pawn, but the manner of his winning it is very impressive.

<table>
<tr><td>

Diagram 116

BLACK

WHITE *to move*
</td><td>

Diagram 117

BLACK *to move*

WHITE
</td></tr>
</table>

WHITE	BLACK		WHITE	BLACK
1 BxN	BxB		1	NxP!
2 NxB	RxN		2 KxN	NxN
3 Q-Q5ch and wins			3 BxN	Q-R5ch and wins

Queen Forks with Checkmate Threats

If Queen forks with checks are more formidable than plain Queen forks, then the double attacks which involve mate threats are even more powerful. The possibility that a player can escape from checkmate and simultaneously salvage one of his attacked men is naturally slight.

In Diagram 118 White, after 1 Q-K4, threatens 2 QxRP mate and also attacks Black's Bishop. Black can stop the mate, but he must lose the Bishop in the process.

Diagram 119 presents a similar attack. If Black tries to parry both threats with 1 ... R-K1 (protecting his Bishop and giving his King a flight-square), the result is 2 QxRPch, K-B1; 3 Q-R8 mate.

Diagram 118
BLACK

WHITE *to move*

WHITE   BLACK
1   Q-K4 and wins

Diagram 119
BLACK

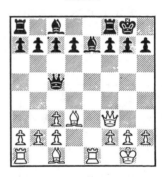

WHITE *to move*

WHITE   BLACK
1   Q-K4 and wins

In Diagram 120 Black is ahead in material with Rook and two Knights against Queen and Pawn. However, White's 1 Q-Q4 threatens 2 Q-N7 mate and also 2 QxN/R7. White must therefore win a piece.

The play leading up to the mate threat in Diagram 121 is highly interesting. Note 4 Q-Q5 threatens 5 QxBP mate and also 5 QxR, not to mention 5 QxB.

An important point to note about all these double attacks is that they are particularly effective where at least one of the targets is an unprotected chessman.

Diagram 120

BLACK

WHITE *to move*

WHITE	BLACK
1 Q-Q4 and wins	

Diagram 121

BLACK

WHITE *to move*

WHITE	BLACK
1 P-KB4	B-Q3
2 P-K5	B-B4ch
3 K-R1	N-N1
4 Q-Q5 and wins	

Rook Forks

These are much less common than Queen forks—not surprisingly, since the Queen is so much more powerful.

In Diagram 122 Black's 1 ... R-N5 leaves White with only one reply if he is to try to save his attacked Bishop. But after 2 QxBP, Black wins White's Queen with 2 ... B-N2.

In Diagram 123 White's 1 R-B5 attacks Black's Bishop, which is undefended, and attacks Black's Knight a second time. Black must lose a piece.

In Diagram 124 Black has to create the proper setting for a Rook fork. It requires imagination and experience to foresee the kind of position in which Black can win a piece by means of a Rook fork.

This applies even more strongly in Diagram 125 where Black's method of winning a piece is quite subtle.

Diagram 122
BLACK *to move*

WHITE

WHITE	BLACK
1	R-N5
2 QxBP	B-N2 and wins

Diagram 123
BLACK

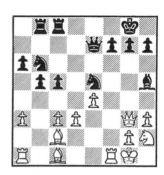

WHITE *to move*

WHITE	BLACK
1 R-B5 and wins	

Diagram 124
BLACK *to move*

WHITE

WHITE	BLACK
1	QxQ
2 RxQ	B-N5
3 R/Q2-Q1	R-B7
	and wins

Diagram 125
BLACK *to move*

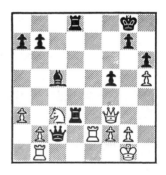

WHITE

WHITE	BLACK
1	QxR/N8ch!
2 NxQ	RxQ
3 PxR	R-Q8ch
	and wins

Bishop Forks

For some reason Bishop forks seem more common than Rook forks. Diagram 126 is a perfect example of a Bishop fork. Black wins a piece, and again we see how vulnerable unprotected targets are to a double attack.

In Diagram 127 we have a classic instance of the way to set up a Bishop fork. Black's preliminary sacrifice of the Exchange nets him a clear piece, as he must win the menaced White Rook.

Diagram 128 shows the same kind of preliminary sacrifice of the Exchange as we had in the previous diagram.

In Diagram 129, however, we have a cleverly prepared Bishop fork which leaves Black a piece ahead, since 4 . . . P-B3! compels White's Queen to renounce the protection of the menaced White Rook.

Pawn Forks

Though the Pawn is the weakest of all the chessmen, a Pawn fork is one of the deadliest stratagems in the whole range of chess.

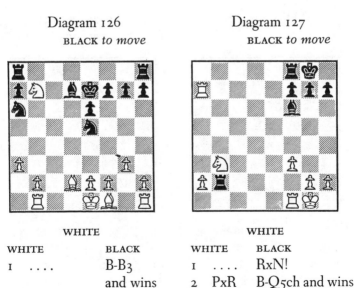

Diagram 126	Diagram 127
BLACK *to move*	BLACK *to move*

WHITE		WHITE	
WHITE	BLACK	WHITE	BLACK
I	B-B3	I	RxN!
	and wins	2 PxR	B-Q5ch and wins

Diagram 128
BLACK *to move*

WHITE

WHITE	BLACK
1	RxB!
2 RxR	BxPch
	and wins

Diagram 129
BLACK *to move*

WHITE

WHITE	BLACK
1	R-K1!
2 Q-KB4	RxN!
3 QxR	B-Q5
4 Q-N5	P-B3!
	and wins

Diagram 130
BLACK

WHITE *to move*

WHITE	BLACK
1 NxB	RxN
2 P-B4 and wins	

Diagram 131
BLACK

WHITE *to move*

WHITE	BLACK
1 Q-K7ch!	KxN
2 P-KN4ch and wins	

Diagram 130 shows a neat Pawn fork which wins a piece.

In Diagram 131 White forces the win of Black's Queen by means of a preliminary Queen check.

Diagram 132 shows how White prepares a Pawn fork against the Black Rooks. If Black declines the offered Pawn, White plays 2 BPxKP with the same result.

In Diagram 133 the double Pawn push of Black's King Knight Pawn results in a Pawn fork which wins a piece.

<table>
<tr><td align="center">Diagram 132</td><td align="center">Diagram 133</td></tr>
<tr><td align="center">BLACK</td><td align="center">BLACK to move</td></tr>
</table>

 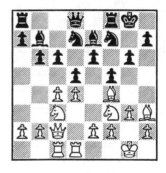

<table>
<tr><td align="center">WHITE to move</td><td align="center">WHITE</td></tr>
</table>

WHITE		BLACK		WHITE		BLACK
1	P-B6ch!	KPxP		1	....	P-KN4!
2	P-K7 and wins			2	B-K3	P-N5 and wins

Knight Forks

Though the Knight fork is a form of double attack, we treat it separately because it is particularly effective and because it is so dreaded by inexperienced players. Awed as they are by the Knight's "peculiar" jump, they find it difficult to visualize the Knight's simultaneous attack in two different directions.

The Knight fork is often prepared by a sacrifice—more accurately, perhaps, a "pseudo-sacrifice." We see this clearly in Diagram 134, where a preliminary Queen sacrifice leads to a Knight fork that leaves White a piece up after 3 NxQ.

Diagram 135 presents an even more interesting situation, as a sacrificial Rook fork paves the way for the ensuing Knight fork.

Diagram 134
BLACK

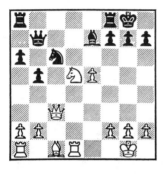

WHITE *to move*

WHITE	BLACK
1 QxN!	QxQ
2 NxBch	K-R1
3 NxQ and wins	

Diagram 135
BLACK

WHITE *to move*

WHITE	BLACK
1 RxPch!	QxR
2 N-K7ch	K moves
3 NxQ and wins	

In the play from the position shown in Diagram 136 White must play 2 KxP in order to prevent Black's King Pawn from queening. This sets the stage for Black's winning Knight fork.

In Diagram 137, on the other hand, we get an immediate Knight fork which allows White to play 2 Q-N4ch (Queen fork) and 3 QxR, with the Exchange ahead.

Black's first move in Diagram 138 forces the win of the Exchange: his Knight attacks White's advanced Rook and also threatens . . . N-Q6 with a fork on White's Bishop and his other Rook. Such is the power of the Knight that White cannot prevent . . . N-Q6 with 2 R-Q7 or 2 R-N3.

The play in Diagram 139 is quite out of the ordinary. If Black answers the astounding Queen sacrifice with 1 . . . RxQ, then 2 RxQch (a Rook fork) wins Black's Bishop.

A series of logical exchanges in Diagram 140 allows White to bring off a Knight fork that will win him the Exchange. Again

Diagram 136
BLACK *to move*

WHITE

WHITE	BLACK
1	N-B6ch
2 K-B1	P-K7ch
3 KxP	N-Q5ch
	and wins

Diagram 137
BLACK

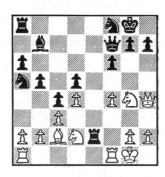

WHITE *to move*

WHITE	BLACK
1 N-R6ch!	PxN
2 Q-N4ch	....
and wins	

Diagram 138
BLACK *to move*

WHITE

WHITE	BLACK
1	N-B4
2 R/N7-N1	N-Q6
	and wins

Diagram 139
BLACK

WHITE *to move*

WHITE	BLACK
1 QxRPch!!	KxQ
2 RxRch	QxR
3 N-B5ch	K moves
4 NxQ and wins	

it takes imagination and experience to see such possibilities.

In Diagram 141 White's preliminary sacrifice of the Exchange leads to a Knight fork that leaves him a piece ahead.

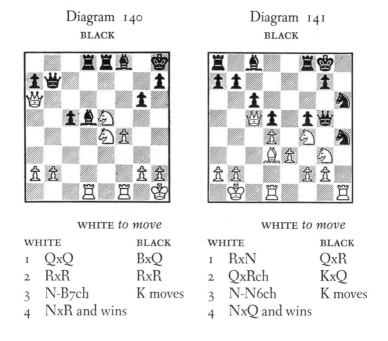

Diagram 140		Diagram 141	
BLACK		**BLACK**	
WHITE *to move*		WHITE *to move*	
WHITE	BLACK	WHITE	BLACK
1 QxQ	BxQ	1 RxN	QxR
2 RxR	RxR	2 QxRch	KxQ
3 N-B7ch	K moves	3 N-N6ch	K moves
4 NxR and wins		4 NxQ and wins	

THE PIN

Earlier we had examples of pins in Diagrams 87 and 104-109.

A pin is an attack on a chessman which screens an even more valuable chessman from attack.

There are two kinds of pins—absolute pins and relative pins.

In the case of an absolute pin, the King is being screened from attack. This means that the pinned piece cannot move, since such a move would be illegal. In the play from Diagram 144, for example, it is clear that Black cannot play 3 . . . PxB, as this would expose his King to attack.

In the case of a relative pin, the protected unit is some chessman other than the King. A move of the pinned man would be legal though usually inadvisable. Thus, in the play arising from Diagram 145, Black can *legally* play 3 ... BxNP, although the move would cost a Rook.

The pin is one of the most popular forms of attack in the whole range of chess tactics. The element of restraint is the secret of its success. The pinned piece is generally helpless against added pressure and, consequently, makes a rewarding target.

Take Diagram 142 as an example. White's 1 R-KN4! comes as a great surprise, since the attacking Rook is unprotected. Yet as the ensuing play demonstrates, capture of the Rook leads to a mate in two. Black's only alternative is to give up his Queen, which only postpones his defeat.

In Diagram 143 White, who is the Exchange ahead, gives up a Rook in order to carry out his attack on the pinned Knight. Subsequently, his 3 B-R6 (threatening 4 Q-N7 mate) leaves Black defenseless.

Diagram 142
BLACK

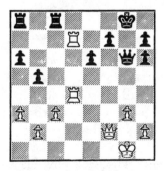

WHITE *to move*

WHITE	BLACK
1 R-KN4!	QxR
2 QxPch	K-R1
3 QxRP mate	

Diagram 143
BLACK

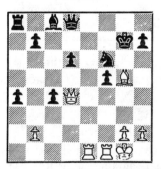

WHITE *to move*

WHITE	BLACK
1 R-K8!	QxR
2 QxNch	K-N1
3 B-R6	Q-B2
4 Q-Q8ch	Q-B1
5 QxQ mate	

One of the true signs of a master is the creation of a pin where it does not yet exist. We are assuming, of course, that opportunities to exploit the pin will be available.

White's task along these lines is rather simple in Diagram 144. His 1 BxN practically points a pistol at Black's head.

In Diagram 145 the play is somewhat more subtle. It takes some imagination to see that Black's Rook on Queen Bishop 1 must be deprived of protection in order to make the ultimate 3 P-N6 effective.

Diagram 144	Diagram 145
BLACK	BLACK

WHITE *to move*   WHITE *to move*

WHITE	BLACK	WHITE	BLACK
1 BxN	QxB	1 NxB	RxN
2 QxQ	PxQ	2 BxN	PxB
3 BxB and wins		3 P-N6 and wins	

In Diagram 146 White's task is easy. His Rook pins Black's Knight, so that 1 B-B4 readily suggests itself by way of bringing more pressure to bear on the unfortunate Knight.

On the other hand, White's play in Diagram 147 has to be of a much higher order. He starts off with a move that is most difficult to find—the Knight fork 1 N-B7! Black naturally plays 1 ... QxN, but now Black's Queen Bishop Pawn is truly pinned, and 2 QxR! neatly exploits the situation, leaving White a clear Exchange ahead.

Diagram 146
BLACK

WHITE *to move*

WHITE	BLACK
1 B-B4 and wins	

Diagram 147
BLACK

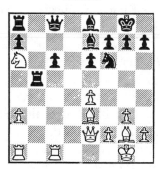

WHITE *to move*

WHITE	BLACK
1 N-B7!	QxN
2 QxR	PxQ
3 RxQ and wins	

Diagram 148
BLACK

WHITE *to move*

WHITE	BLACK
1 RxN	PxR
2 R-N1 and wins	

Diagram 149
BLACK *to move*

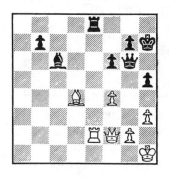

WHITE

WHITE	BLACK
1	QxPch!
2 QxQ	RxR
3 QxB	PxQ and wins

Often the presence of King and Queen on the same line will give us pinning ideas. This is the case in Diagram 148, where Black's King and Queen are both on the King Knight file. This inspires White to sacrifice the Exchange in order to open the file and thereby create the possibility of pinning Black's Queen.

Diagram 149 shows how a pinned piece loses its protective function. After 2 . . . RxR, White has nothing better than 3 QxB, leaving Black with a decisive material advantage.

The way Black turns the tables in Diagram 150 is very neat. At first sight it seems that White's pin must be deadly, but Black's 1 . . . RxB! enables him to set up a pin of his own. Note that in the subsequent play (after 2 RxR, Q-QN2; 3 Q-KN2) Black would blunder grossly if he played 3 . . . N-B5? (a faulty Knight fork), because 4 R-Q8ch! would lead to the loss of Black's Queen. Instead Black forces the win by very precise play.

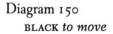

Diagram 150	Diagram 151
BLACK *to move*	BLACK *to move*

 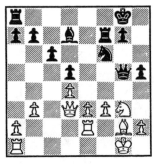

WHITE	WHITE

WHITE	BLACK	WHITE	BLACK
1	RxB!	1	P-R5
2 RxR	Q-QN2	2 N-B1	P-R6
3 Q-KN2	Q-N8ch!		and wins
4 Q-N1	Q-K5ch!		
5 Q-N2	QxQch		
6 KxQ	N-B5ch		
7 K moves	NxR and wins		

In Diagram 151 Black creates a winning pin by the advance of his King Rook Pawn. Here the presence of White's King and Black's Queen on the same file gives us the winning idea. White's unfortunate pinned Bishop pays the penalty.

From what we have so far learned about pins, we might get the idea that they must infallibly win the game. This is not so. There are occasions when they can be broken profitably, and such occasions should be exploited alertly.

Diagram 152 is a case in point. Black's game seems to be in ruins, and yet he has a winning move.

In Diagram 153 we get the impression that White, with his pieces powerfully posted and with a material advantage of two Pawns, can win almost as he pleases. But again Black upsets the applecart by forcibly removing the pinning piece.

Diagram 152	Diagram 153
BLACK *to move*	BLACK *to move*

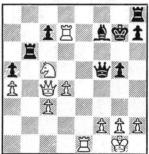

WHITE   WHITE

WHITE	BLACK	WHITE	BLACK
1	QxRch!	1	QxR!
2 KxQ	PxQ	2 NxQ	BxQ
	and wins		and wins

OVERWORKED PIECES

An overworked piece is one which has two jobs to do at the same time. Attack this overworked piece and you make it impossible for this protective unit to continue doing all the work that has been assigned to it.

Take Diagram 154 as an example. Black's Rook has the job of preventing White from playing RxN mate. But when White plays 1 Q-B4!! he threatens 2 Q-N8 mate. So now Black's Rook has the task of preventing two different mates and, consequently, becomes overworked.

Diagram 155 shows Black's Queen as the overworked piece. As you can see, Black's Queen and his Rook at King 2 have the function of preventing a mate beginning with 1 QxNPch, etc. However, by playing 1 R-B8ch! White turns the Black Queen into an intolerably overworked piece. White is then able to engineer the mate he originally had in mind.

<table>
<tr><td>Diagram 154</td><td>Diagram 155</td></tr>
<tr><td>BLACK</td><td>BLACK</td></tr>
</table>

<table>
<tr><td>WHITE to move</td><td>WHITE to move</td></tr>
</table>

WHITE	BLACK		WHITE	BLACK
1 Q-B4!	RxQ		1 R-B8ch!	QxR
2 RxN mate			2 QxNPch!	RxQ
			3 RxR mate	

Diagram 156 presents a mating theme of singular beauty, previously illustrated in the play from Diagram 75. When White plays 1 Q-K7! it turns out that Black's Rook at King Bishop 2 is an overworked piece, since 1 . . . RxQ cannot be played because it leads to a 2 R-B8 mate. (The similarity of Diagram 75 and

Diagram 156 shows how we can use similar patterns to good advantage in our own games.) In view of the pressure on Black's game it is not surprising that White succeeds in carrying out his idea.

The play from Diagram 157 is a very straightforward affair. Black's Rook at King Rook 3 has the task of preventing B-N6 mate. By playing 1 Q-R5ch! White turns this Rook into an overworked piece. This enables the White Bishop to deliver checkmate.

Diagram 156
BLACK

Diagram 157
BLACK

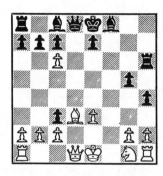

WHITE *to move*   WHITE *to move*

WHITE	BLACK	WHITE	BLACK
1 Q-K7!	Q-B2	1 Q-R5ch!	RxQ
2 Q-B8ch	RxQ	2 B-N6 mate	
3 RxR mate			

In Diagram 158 White's Queen has the task of defending the White Pawn at King Bishop 3. With the unexpected double attack 1 ... R-Q7! Black converts the White Queen into an overworked piece. White cannot achieve the double object of saving his Bishop *and* the King Bishop Pawn. Consequently, after 2 QxR, NxP, we find that Black threatens 3 ... QxRP mate and also 3 ... NxQ. White is lost, as he cannot defend himself against both threats. He must, therefore, lose his Queen.

In Diagram 159 Black's position is menacing, but there seems to be no direct threat. However, after 1 ... R-K7! (threatening mate), we find that White's Rook at King 1 is sadly overburdened. This Rook "wants" to play 2 RxR to stop the mate, but it also has the duty of protecting its fellow Rook. There is no satisfactory way for White to get out of this cruel dilemma.

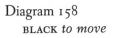

Diagram 158
BLACK *to move*

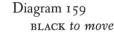

Diagram 159
BLACK *to move*

WHITE

WHITE

WHITE	BLACK
1	R-Q7!
2 QxR	NxP and wins

WHITE	BLACK
1	R-K7!
2 RxR	QxR mate

REMOVING THE GUARD

This theme is very similar to the previous one. Where a chessman is tied to a protective function, the logical course is to knock out the defensive unit. With the completion of this stroke the opponent's position will collapse.

Diagram 160 is a perfect illustration of this procedure. Black's King Pawn and Bishop guard his advanced Knight. By removing both guards, White wins a piece with 3 BxN or 3 QxN.

Again, in Diagram 161 Black's Queen protects his Knight (which, by the way, is pinned). By 1 R-K8! White forces Black's Queen away from the defense, with catastrophic consequences for Black.

Diagram 162 illustrates a procedure which is very common and

Diagram 160

BLACK

WHITE *to move*

WHITE	BLACK
1 PxP	QxP
2 NxB	
and wins	

Diagram 161

BLACK

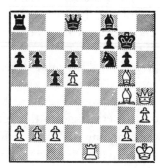

WHITE *to move*

WHITE	BLACK
1 R-K8!	QxR
2 BxNch	K-N1
3 Q-R8 mate	

Diagram 162

BLACK

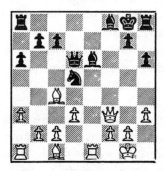

WHITE *to move*

WHITE	BLACK
1 RxB!	QxR
2 BxN and wins	

Diagram 163

BLACK

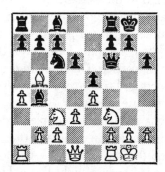

WHITE *to move*

WHITE	BLACK
1 N-Q5	Q-Q1
2 BxN	PxB
3 NxB and wins	

very powerful. White attacks Black's Knight twice, and in turn Black gives the Knight twofold protection. But when White removes one of the guards with 1 RxB! Black's game collapses, and on the next move he not only loses the Knight but finds his Queen in a fatal pin.

It may not be immediately apparent in Diagram 163 that Black's Knight is the guard that must be removed if White is to win the exposed Bishop at his Queen Knight 4. The winning process is crisp and to the point.

In Diagram 164 White's King guards the White Queen. It is a simple matter to force the White King away, so that the Queen must be lost.

In Diagram 165 White's Bishop is guarded not once but twice. Yet Black can remove both guards and thereby succeed in winning the Bishop. Note, by the way, that Black's first two moves can be transposed.

DEFENSIVE COMBINATIONS

The combinations we have seen can help you add enormously to your chessplaying skill if you master them so that you can recognize the patterns in your own games and turn the winning stratagems to good account. It would be a mistake, however, to assume that these patterns must *always* win.

There are times when even the most formidable-looking attack can be parried. Defense offers rewarding scope to the player who is alert and resourceful. By the same token despair merely means premature surrender.

For a splendid example of defensive resourcefulness, consider the situation in Diagram 166. Black's Bishop is pinned and apparently lost. But Black has a powerful resource in his far advanced Queen Knight Pawn. He can play 1 . . . B-R7!?; 2 RxRch, RxR; 3 RxRch, K-R2; 4 R-QN8 (or 4 R-Q1), P-N8/Q; 5 RxQ, BxR; and the ending is a draw.

But Black has a better idea: 1 . . . B-N6!; 2 RxRch, RxR and now White must not play 3 RxRch? because after 3 . . . K-R2, he cannot stop the advanced Pawn from queening. White would

Diagram 164		Diagram 165	
BLACK *to move*		BLACK *to move*	

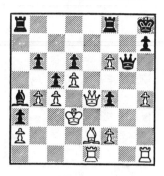

WHITE

WHITE

WHITE	BLACK	WHITE	BLACK
1	B-B7ch	1	BxN
2 KxB	QxQch	2 PxB	P-KN4
	and wins	3 N moves	RxB and wins

have to play 4 R-QN1, and after 4 ... BxP; 5 RxP, B-N4; Black would have winning chances because of his extra Pawn.

But even this line of play is not the last word, as Black could try: 1 ... P-K4! If White replies 2 BxP, there follows 2 ... R-B8, and Black's far advanced Pawn must queen. Consequently, after 1 ... P-K4! White replies 2 RxB, RxR; 3 PxR, PxB; 4 R-QN1. But then comes 4 ... R-B7ch; 5 K-K1, R-B8ch; and Black queens his Pawn after all.

It turns out, then, that in the position of Diagram 166, despite all appearances to the contrary, Black has a clear win!

In a way Diagram 167 is even more remarkable. On the face of it Black wins at once with his threat of ... Q-R7 mate. White's 1 R-K8ch looks like sheer desperation; note, however, that 1 ... K-R2 will not do because White would reply 2 Q-Q3ch (double attack) winning the Black Rook. Black, therefore, replies 1 ... B-B1, but this enables White to uncover a magnificent resource that wins the game.

It would be difficult to find a situation drearier than White's position in Diagram 168. In addition to being a piece down, he

Diagram 166
BLACK *to move*

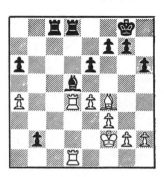

WHITE

Diagram 167
BLACK

WHITE *to move*

WHITE		BLACK
1	....	P-K4!
2	RxB	RxR
3	PxR	PxB
4	R-QN1	R-B7ch
5	K-K1	R-B8ch
		and wins

WHITE		BLACK
1	R-K8ch	B-B1
2	RxBch!	KxR
3	N-B5 dis ch	K-N1
4	Q-B8ch!!	KxQ
5	R-Q8 mate	

is menaced by a triple fork of the Black Knight. However, 1 Q-B6! (threatening 2 Q-N7 mate) wins at once.

Diagram 169 confronts us with a very critical situation. Though White is a piece and a Pawn ahead, his game is in serious danger because his attacked Queen cannot retreat (1 Q-B3?, QxP mate).

If White tries 1 Q-N7ch, QxQ; 2 RxQ, KxR; he is the Exchange down with a lost game.

Does it then follow that White is irretrievably lost? No, for he can save himself with 1 R-N5!

If Black replies 1 ... QxR, then White wins easily with 2 QxRch and 3 QxP, etc. Or if Black plays 1 ... RxQ, then White still wins easily with 2 RxQ. (Of course, Black dare not play 1 ... Q-K3?? or 1 ... Q-B5?? because of 2 Q-N7 mate.)

However, in reply to 1 R-N5! Black has a splendid resource in 1 ... R-K1 (for if 2 RxQ?, R-K8 mate). After 1 ... R-K1, Black is threatening mate and also threatening 2 ... QxR.

There is only one safe parry for White: 2 R-N1 guarding
against both threats. But Black replies 2 ... R-KN1, returning
to the diagram position. White must again try 3 R-N5, and the
outcome is a draw by repetition of moves.

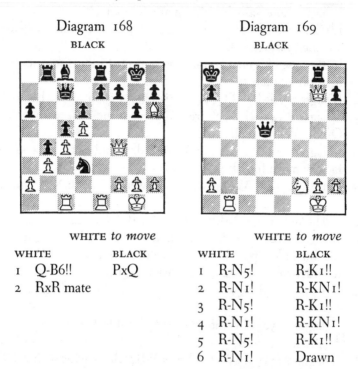

Diagram 168	Diagram 169
BLACK	BLACK
WHITE *to move*	WHITE *to move*

WHITE	BLACK	WHITE	BLACK
1 Q-B6!!	PxQ	1 R-N5!	R-K1!!
2 RxR mate		2 R-N1!	R-KN1!
		3 R-N5!	R-K1!!
		4 R-N1!	R-KN1!
		5 R-N5!	R-K1!!
		6 R-N1!	Drawn

In this chapter we have seen many ways to win material as well
as additional ways to force mate. There is a wealth of information
here to help the student improve his game, as these patterns recur
repeatedly.

We have also learned earlier that by winning material we are
on the way to winning the game. For, as has been stated repeatedly, *superior force wins*. Being a piece ahead spells out an
advantage so great that the win almost plays itself. Winning a
Pawn, on the other hand, is not only much more common, it is also
much more difficult to convert into a win. So it is to this type of
advantage that we shall turn our attention in Chapter 5.

SEVENTH REVIEW TEST
(answers on pages 103–104)

1. A _____ is an attack on a chessman which screens an even more valuable chessman from attack.

2. In the case of an _____ pin, the King is being screened from attack.

3. In the case of a relative pin, the protected unit is some chessman other than the _____.

4. [Diagram 142] 1 R-Q8ch (is/is not) a good move. Reason?

5. [Diagram 143] If Black tries to prevent the mate with 3 ... Q-N3, White replies 4 _____.

6. [Diagram 144] 1 ... PxB (would/would not) be a satisfactory move for Black. Reason?

7. [Diagram 145] White would answer 3 ... BxNP with 4 _____.

8. [Diagram 147] 1 N-B7! forks both Black _____.

9. [Diagram 148] The fact that Black's King and Queen are on the same file gives White the idea of sacrificing the Exchange in order to _____ Black's Queen.

10. [Diagram 149] 3 QxR (would/would not) be an illegal move. Reason?

11. [Diagram 150] If White plays 3 Q-R5, Black wins with 3 ... _____ or 3 ... _____.

12. [Diagram 151] If White plays 2 P-B4, Black wins with 2 ... _____, intending to answer 3 N-B1 with 3 ... _____.

13. [Diagram 152] If Black plays 1 ... P-N4, White replies 2 _____.

14. An _____ piece is one which has two jobs to do at the same time.

15. [Diagram 155] White can also win with 1 R-B7, for if Black replies 1 ... RxR, there follows 2 _____, _____; 3 _____ mate.

16. [Diagram 156] If Black plays 1 ... RxR, White replies 2 _____.

17. [Diagram 157] Black (can/cannot) play 1 ... K-Q2. Reason?

18. [Diagram 158] If White plays 2 Q-K3, Black wins with 2 ... —————; 3 —————, —————; 4 —————, —————; 5 —————, —————; etc.

19. [Diagram 159] When Black plays 1 ... R-K7! he is threatening 2 ... ————— or 2 ... —————.

20. [Diagram 162] If Black plays 1 ... Q-Q2, White's strongest reply is 2 —————.

21. [Diagram 163] If the continuation is 1 ... Q-N3; 2 BxN, PxB; White then continues with 3 —————.

22. [Diagram 165] If play proceeds 1 ... P-KN4; 2 N/B4-Q5; Black can win a piece with 2 ... —————. Reason?

23. [Diagram 166] After Black plays 3 ... PxB, he threatens to win at once with 4 ... —————.

24. [Diagram 167] If Black plays 4 ... K-R2, White replies 5 —————.

25. [Diagram 168] Assume that Black's Bishop is at Queen 2. Then if White plays 1 Q-B6, Black replies 1 ... ————— winning.

26. If White plays 1 R-Q1 in the position of Diagram 169, Black replies 1 ... ————— and wins, as he comes out the Exchange ahead.

Seventh Review Test: Answers

1. pin
2. absolute
3. King
4. is not; White loses a Rook after 1 ... RxR; 2 RxRch, RxR; etc.
5. Q-B8 mate
6. would not; White replies

2 RxQ with a winning material advantage
7. RxRch
8. Rooks
9. pin
10. would; 3 QxR would expose White's King to attack by the Black Bishop

11. N-B2 or N-B5
12. Q-N5; P-R6
13. Q-N7 mate
14. overworked
15. Q-K8ch, K-R2; R-KR3 mate
16. Q-N7 mate
17. cannot; ... K-Q2 would expose the Black King to attack by White's Pawn at Queen Bishop 6
18. RxBP; R-N2, RxR; KxR, Q-R6ch; K-R1, NxP; Q-K2, R-K1; etc.
19. QxRP mate or Q-N7 mate

20. BxN
21. N-K7ch winning the Black Queen
22. BxN/Q4; if White replies 2 NxB, Black can .play 2 ... RxB; or if White plays 2 RxB, then 2 ... BxN; 3 PxB, RxB wins for Black
23. R-B8
24. Q-N7 mate
25. PxQ (Black's back rank is protected)
26. QxRch!

CHAPTER 5

SUPERIOR FORCE WINS: SIMPLE ENDGAMES

THE ENDGAME is just what its name implies. It is the final phase where all accounts are settled. It is, in the most important practical sense, the stage at which a Pawn advantage is important.

Why so? The endgame is a necessarily simplified stage when most of the pieces (above all, the Queens) have disappeared from the board. The king, which in the early stages had to be carefully guarded and shielded, now becomes a powerful unit. He is free to protect his own Pawns and menace hostile Pawns.

Why is this important? Because the endgame revolves about the attempted *queening of a Pawn*. If the Pawn, generally an extra Pawn, can be converted into a Queen, it then becomes possible to force checkmate in the basic mate of King and Queen against lone King. *Thus it follows that a player who is a Pawn ahead is potentially a Queen ahead.*

We can realize the importance of this point from studying Diagrams 170 and 171. In Diagram 170 White is ahead in material, but he cannot force checkmate—King and Bishop are unable to force checkmate.

In Diagram 171, however, the situation is quite different. White has a Pawn which can be converted into a Queen; he must, therefore, win. Play might proceed in the following manner:

	WHITE	BLACK
1	B-N4	K-B2
2	BxPch	K-K2
3	BxP	K-Q2
4	B-K4	K-K2
5	P-Q5	K-Q2
6	P-Q6	K-Q1
7	K-K6	K-K1
8	P-Q7ch	K-Q1
9	B-Q5	K-B2
10	K-K7	K-N1
11	P-Q8/Qch	

And White mates shortly.

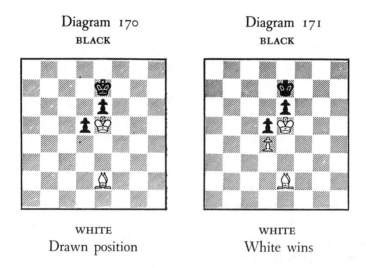

Diagram 170
BLACK

WHITE
Drawn position

Diagram 171
BLACK

WHITE
White wins

That White should win in the position shown in Diagram 171 comes as no great surprise, since he is a Bishop ahead. But that it is possible to win with a "mere" King and Pawn against King seems remarkable. And in fact it *is* remarkable. These endings, "simple" as they are in appearance, combine delicacy and force with noteworthy effectiveness.

BASIC KING AND PAWN ENDINGS

In these endings the principle of the "Opposition" is of great importance. See Diagram 172, which illustrates the point effectively.

We say that the two Kings are in Opposition when they face each other on the same line, separated by an odd number of squares. Opposition, then, may take place on a file, rank, or diagonal. For practical purposes the Opposition on a file is by far the most important.

The player whose King does *not* have to move is said to have the Opposition. Having the Opposition will often assure a favorable outcome. Not having it will generally lead to loss. An example of this is given in Diagram 172.

The two Kings face each other in Opposition. It is Black's turn to move. Therefore, White has the Opposition and will win. Play proceeds:

	WHITE	BLACK
1	....	K-K1
2	P-K7	K-B2
3	K-Q7	....

Diagram 172
BLACK *to move*

WHITE
White wins

Diagram 173
BLACK *to move*

WHITE
White wins

White queens his Pawn, with an easy win. We can derive an important practical rule here: *The player with the extra Pawn will win if he has the Opposition after his Pawn has advanced to the sixth rank.*

But we have not yet exhausted the possibilities of Diagram 172. Suppose *White* moves first. What then? In that case the position is drawn:

WHITE	BLACK
1 P-K7ch	K-K1

Now White has only one move to protect his Pawn.

2 K-K6	Drawn

Black is stalemated!

Second rule: *If the Pawn gives check on advancing to the seventh rank, the position is a draw.*

But, you may ask, doesn't White have any alternative method? Can he maneuver with a view to seizing the Opposition? Let's see:

WHITE	BLACK
1 K-Q5	K-K2
2 K-K5	. . . .

And now if Black plays 2 ... K-Q1?? White replies 3 K-Q6, seizing the Opposition and winning.

2	K-K1!
3 K-Q6	K-Q1

The position is still a draw.

In Diagram 173 White would win easily if it were his move. He would simply play 1 P-K6, giving us the situation shown in Diagram 172.

But the stated condition in Diagram 173 is that it is Black's move. White still wins:

WHITE	BLACK
1	K-K1

Now if White plays 2 P-K6?? Black plays 2 ... K-Q1 and draws.

Instead, *White wins by seizing the Opposition.*

2 K-K6!	K-Q1

Or 2 ... K-B1; 3 K-Q7, etc. In either case Black loses the Opposition, which forces him to allow White to control the queening square.

3 K-B7	....

This·settles the matter. With White in control of the queening square, White will soon have a Queen.

3	K-Q2
4 P-K6ch	K-Q1
5 P-K7ch	K moves
·6 P-K8/Q	....

And White forces mate.

In Diagram 174 White has an easy win, for he can maintain the Opposition by moving his Pawn.

WHITE	BLACK
1 P-K4!	K-Q2

If Black plays 1 ... K-B2, then White replies 2 K-Q6 with a similar result.

2 K-B6	K-K1
3 P-K5	K-B1
4 P-K6	K-K1
5 P-K7	

And White soon queens his Pawn.

Of course, if Black moves first in the position shown in Diagram 174, then the win is even easier, as Black must give up the Opposition with his very first move.

Diagram 174
BLACK

WHITE *to move*
White wins

Diagram 175
BLACK *to move*

WHITE
Drawn position

Diagram 175 presents an extremely instructive position. Even though Black has to lose the Opposition, he still draws because he can always get back the Opposition at a later, critical stage. At first sight this seems to be an exception to our rules. But it really is not; the drawback to White's situation is that *his King is not in front of the Pawn and that he is, therefore, not in a position to seize the Opposition at critical junctures.*

WHITE	BLACK
1	K-K4
2 P-K4	. . . .

If Black now makes the mistake of playing 2 . . . K-B5?? then White gets the Opposition for keeps with 3 K-Q4! (On 3 . . . K-N4 White will play 4 K-K5! maintaining the Opposition *in front of the Pawn.*)

2	....	K-K3
3	K-Q4	K-Q3

Black maintains the Opposition so that the White King has no effective point of entry.

4	P-K5ch	K-K3
5	K-K4	K-K2
6	K-Q5	....

Now 6 ... K-B2?? allows White to get the Opposition by 7 K-Q6, K-K1; 8 K-K6 and wins.

6	....	K-Q2!
7	P-K6ch	K-K1!

Note that 7 ... K-Q1?? loses to 8 K-Q6, giving White the Opposition (Diagram 172).

· 8	K-K5	....

If 8 K-Q6, K-Q1!, Black draws, as he has the Opposition.

8	....	K-K2!

Black must not play 8 ... K-Q1?? allowing White to take the Opposition (9 K-Q6) and win.

9	K-B5	K-K1!

And here 9 ... K-B1?? loses to 10 K-B6, etc.

10	K-B6	K-B1!

White cannot win (11 P-K7ch, K-K1; 12 K-K6; and Black is stalemated).

Another general type of drawn position appears in Diagram 176. Here we note that the Rook Pawn is an exception to the rule that positions on the order of Diagram 174 are always a win.

Study Diagram 176. Move all the forces one file to the right, and the position is an easy win. The situation in Diagram 176 is, however, a draw. This comes about because the White King, being placed at the edge of the board, is unable to move diagonally to the *left* to control the queening square. Again, because the Black King is at the edge of the board, he runs into a stalemate position because of the impossibility of moving aside from the queening square. A draw, then, is inevitable. Here is how the play goes from Diagram 176:

	WHITE	BLACK
1	P-R5	K-N1
2	K-N6	K-R1
3	P-R6	K-N1
4	P-R7ch	K-R1
5	K-R6	Drawn

Black is stalemated.

Diagram 176
BLACK

WHITE *to move*
Drawn position

Diagram 177
BLACK

WHITE *to move*
White wins

MORE KING AND PAWN ENDINGS

Now we come to King and Pawn endings which, though they are not basic, nevertheless, embody principles that are well worth knowing.

Diagram 177, for example, shows a race to promote Pawns. Both players get new Queens, but White wins because he queens first:

	WHITE	BLACK
1	P-R5	P-N5
2	P-R6	P-N6
3	P-R7	P-N7
4	P-R8/Q	P-N8/Q
5	Q-KN8ch	K moves
6	QxQ and wins	

In Diagram 178 we have an extraordinarily interesting situation in which White wins because he has the Opposition. Black's King must give way, allowing the successful invasion by White's King. We can see that 1 ... K-B3 is altogether out of the question, for then 2 K-Q5 leads to the win of Black's Queen Knight Pawn, followed by the advance of White's newly passed Pawn, long before Black can carry out a similar tactic on the other wing

	WHITE	BLACK
1	....	K-Q3
2	K-Q4	K-K3

Again, note that 2 ... K-B3; 3 K-K5 is much worse for Black.

3	K-B5	K-K4
4	KxP	K-B5
5	K-B4	KxP
6	P-N5	K-R6
7	P-N6	P-N5

8	P-N7	P-N6
9	P-N8/Q	P-N7

See Diagram 179. Though White is a Queen ahead, the win is not easy. White must force the Black King *in front of the Pawn* to prevent it from queening. Each time this happens, White has time to bring his King to the scene of the action.

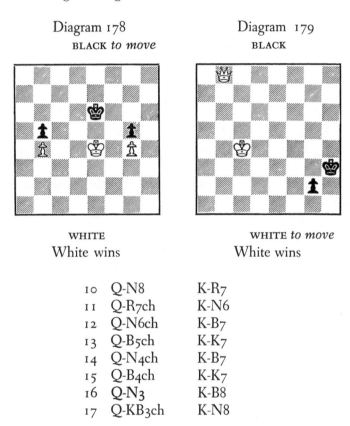

Diagram 178
BLACK *to move*

WHITE
White wins

Diagram 179
BLACK

WHITE *to move*
White wins

10	Q-N8	K-R7
11	Q-R7ch	K-N6
12	Q-N6ch	K-B7
13	Q-B5ch	K-K7
14	Q-N4ch	K-B7
15	Q-B4ch	K-K7
16	Q-N3	K-B8
17	Q-KB3ch	K-N8

White has completed the first part of his task. Now his King can approach, for reasons that will soon become clear.

18	K-Q3	K-R7
19	Q-B2	K-R8

20	Q-R4ch	K-N8

Note that 21 K-K2?? would now stalemate Black.

21	K-K3!	....

Another way is 21 K-Q2!, K-B8; 22 Q-K1 mate.

21	....	K-B8
22	Q-B2 mate	

The outside passed Pawn often represents the margin of victory in a King and Pawn ending. A passed Pawn is one which can advance without fear of hostile Pawns on neighboring files. If it is to be stopped in this type of ending, it must be stopped by the hostile King. If he is not in easy reaching distance of the passed Pawn, he cannot prevent the Pawn from queening.

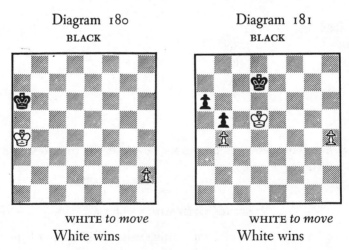

Diagram 180
BLACK

WHITE *to move*
White wins

Diagram 181
BLACK

WHITE *to move*
White wins

In Diagram 180, for example, White's King Rook Pawn is an outside passed Pawn. This enables White to win:

WHITE	BLACK
1 P-R4	K-N3

2	P-R5	K-B3
3	P-R6	K-Q3
4	P-R7	K-K2

Too little and too late.

5	P-R8/Q and wins

Diagram 181 shows how the outside passed Pawn can be effective in enticing the hostile King away from a critical sector. Black's King must keep an eye on White's Rook Pawn, which is an outside passed Pawn. This allows White's King to massacre the Black Pawns:

	WHITE	BLACK
1	P-R5	K-K2
2	P-R6	K-B2

Black has no choice.

3	K-B6	K-N3
4	K-N6	KxP
5	KxP	K-N3
6	KxP	....

White wins easily, as he cannot be prevented from queening his remaining Pawn.

ENDINGS WITH MINOR PIECES

As we know from the table of relative values, Bishop and Knight are of equal value. Nevertheless, in many types of endgames the Bishop has a slight but perceptible advantage in mobility. When this advantage is combined with other favorable factors, it will often tip the scales in favor of the Bishop.

Diagram 182 provides a good example. Here we find that the Black Bishop has a magnificent diagonal and a strong pressure on

White's weak Queen Knight Pawn. The White Knight, on the other hand, is tied down to the defense of the weak Pawn.

In addition, we observe that Black's King is poised for invasion, whereas White's King is limited to defensive functions. Black has the initiative and the mobility needed for victory:

WHITE	BLACK
1	P-B6!

If White plays 2 NxP, there follows 2 ... BxN; 3 PxB, K-B5; 4 K-Q2, K-N6; 5 K-Q3, KxP; and Black wins by advancing his Queen Rook Pawn to the queening square.

	WHITE	BLACK
2	PxP	K-B5
3	K-Q2	K-N6
4	P-R4	KxP
5	K-B2	K-N4
6	N-K3	B-K2!

The Bishop is headed for a new powerful post at Queen Bishop 4. Black has a formidable passed Queen Rook Pawn, while White's Queen Bishop Pawn is weak.

	WHITE	BLACK
7	N-Q1	B-B4!
8	K-N3	P-R5ch
9	K-N2	K-B5
10	K-R2	P-R6

White's King is tied down by the hostile Queen Rook Pawn, and White's Knight is tied down to the defense of his Queen Bishop Pawn.

	WHITE	BLACK
11	K-N1	K-N6
12	K-R1	K-B7!
13	N-K3ch	BxN
14	PxB	KxP
	Resigns	

White resigns because after 15 K-R2, K-Q6; 16 KxP, KxP; Black wins all the King-side Pawns.

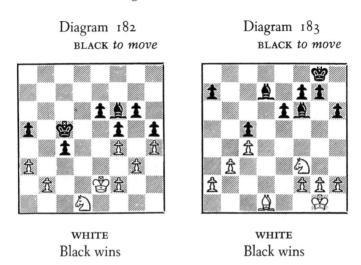

Diagram 182
BLACK *to move*

WHITE
Black wins

Diagram 183
BLACK *to move*

WHITE
Black wins

An ending with two Bishops against Bishop and Knight often illustrates the power of the combined Bishops. Operating together they can control all the squares on the board, and they often do an effective job cutting off useful squares from the opposing Knight's range. Progressive paralysis then turns out to be the Knight's fate. Here is how the play proceeds from Diagram 183:

WHITE	BLACK
1	B-B6!

This prevents White from playing N-Q2 or N-K1. Compare the previous comment on this point.

2	B-B2	B-QB3
3	K-B1	P-B4
4	K-K2	K-B2
5	P-N3	K-B3
6	N-Q2	P-K4

Black intends to convert his four Pawns to three on the King-side into a passed Pawn. White hopes to get a passed Pawn on the other wing, but he cannot succeed.

7	N-N1	B-N5
8	P-QR3	B-R4
9	P-B3	P-R4!
10	B-Q1	P-N4!
11	K-Q3	P-K5ch!

If White captures this Pawn, he loses a piece.

12	K-K3	PxP
13	BxP	BxB
14	KxB	K-K4

Now Black has a straightforward ending of Bishop against Knight in which the Bishop has much greater mobility.

15	K-K3	P-N5!
16	K-Q3	P-B5!

Black is making good progress in forcing a passed Pawn.

17	PxPch	KxP

Now Black is sure of getting a passed Pawn with ... P-R5 and ... P-N6.

18	N-Q2	BxN

Simplifying into a won King and Pawn ending.

19	KxB	....

Now White hopes to get a passed Pawn with P-N4.

19   ....   P-R4!

Preventing P-N4, etc.

20   K-B3   ....

White once more hopes for P-N4, but Black parries alertly on the other wing.

20   ....   P-KR5!
21   K-Q2   P-R6!
22   K-K1   P-N6!
23   PxPch   KxP
24   K-B1   P-R7
      Resigns

Diagram 184
BLACK *to move*

WHITE
Black wins

Diagram 185
BLACK

WHITE *to move*
White wins

Diagram 184 presents the kind of situation in which a Knight is superior to a Bishop. Every White Pawn is on a white square —the same color the Bishop travels on. This means that the Bishop's mobility is hampered by his own Pawns, that the Bishop is limited to defensive play, and that the black squares in White's camp are at the mercy of Black's King and Knight. Follow the play from Diagram 184:

WHITE	BLACK
1	P-R5!

Obviously this Pawn must not be captured.

| 2 B-Q1 | PxP |

And now if 3 BxP, Black replies 3 ... N-Q2 followed by 4 ... N-N3, winning easily.

| 3 PxP | .... |

Now White's Queen Knight Pawn has to be protected by the Bishop instead of by a Pawn.

3	N-Q6!
4 B-K2	N-B5
5 B-B1	N-R4!
6 B-K2	N-N6

The Knight is doing magnificent work on the black squares. Black threatens 7 ... NxB; 8 KxN, K-B6, which would win. Note the aggressive position of Black's King.

7 B-Q3	P-R4!
8 B-N1	P-R5
9 B-Q3	P-KB4
10 B-N1	P-N4
11 B-Q3	P-B5

Now all of White's Pawns are fixed on their squares. The end is nigh.

| 12 B-N1 | N-B8ch! |
| 13 K-K2 | N-K6! |

A very agile Knight.

14   K-B2   K-B6
     Resigns

White is helpless. A great ending.

In Diagram 185 we see a struggle between two Bishops. The issue is decided here by the position of the Pawns. Black has two weak Pawns—one on Queen Rook 4 and one on Queen Bishop 4. These Pawns are not protected by Pawns and must, therefore, be protected by the Black Bishop. White's Bishop attacks; Black's Bishop defends. Sooner or later Black's position must collapse because of this qualitative differential in the two camps. Here is how White wins in Diagram 185:

WHITE	BLACK
1 K-B1	. . . .

White's King heads for Queen Bishop 4 in order to menace Black's weak Pawn. Black's King rushes to defend.

1	. . . .	K-B2
2	K-K2	K-K3
3	K-Q3	P-B4
4	P-B3	P-B5
5	K-B4	K-Q3
6	B-K1!	P-N4
7	B-B2	. . . .

White has the desired position.

7	. . . .	B-N3
8	P-B3!	P-R4
9	P-N4!	. . . .

Black's Pawn at Queen Bishop 4 is pinned on the diagonal.

9	....	RPxP
10	PxP	B-R2
11	P-R5!	....

White is not interested in playing 11 BxPch, BxB; 12 PxBch —or 11 PxPch—as the resulting double Pawn gives him no winning chances. He must, therefore, bring about a position in which Black either (a) has to move his King away or (b) has to remove his Bishop from the critical diagonal.

11	....	P-N5
12	P-R4	P-N6
13	B-N1	B-N1
14	BxPch	Resigns

For after 14 ... K-B2, White wins with 15 P-R6, etc.

ROOK AND PAWN ENDINGS

These are perhaps the commonest of all endgames. Mobility is the key concept in these endings; frequently the superiority in Rook mobility will compensate for the loss of a Pawn. First we deal with two basic endgames, beginning with Diagram 186.

Here White is a Pawn ahead, but his problem—how to queen this Pawn—appears to be a difficult one. He starts by driving off Black's King:

WHITE		BLACK
1	R-QB1ch	K-N2

One would now expect White to play 2 K-Q7 with a view to queening his Pawn, but it's not that easy. There follows 2 ... R-Q7ch; 3 K-K6, R-K7ch; 4 K-Q6, R-Q7ch; 5 K-K5, R-K7ch. White cannot escape from the Rook checks because his King has to stay near the Pawn.

2	R-B4!	R-B8

3	K-Q7	R-Q8ch
4	K-K6	R-K8ch

Black's Rook continues with the nuisance checks, but this time White has a way out, thanks to his 2 R-B4!

5	K-B6	R-KB8ch
6	K-K5	R-K8ch
7	R-K4!	

The point. Black's checks are at an end, and the Pawn must queen.

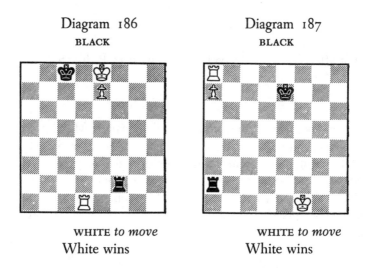

Diagram 186   Diagram 187
BLACK   BLACK

WHITE *to move*   WHITE *to move*
White wins   White wins

In Diagram 187 White is a Pawn ahead, but it seems that he has no way of putting it to use. Black's Rook menaces the Pawn from the rear, tying White's Rook to the defense of the Pawn. Nevertheless, White can win by a neat trick:

	WHITE	BLACK
1	R-KR8!	RxP

Forced.

	2	R-R7ch	....

This "skewer" wins Black's Rook. After Black's King moves, White plays 3 RxR and then forces the basic checkmate of King and Rook against King.

Now we come to somewhat more involved endings taken from actual play. In Diagram 188 Black has a decided advantage in the form of the passed Queen Bishop Pawn. This is the "superior force," even though the players are mathematically even in material. Observe also that Black's King is right in the middle of the battle, whereas White's King is shut off.

WHITE	BLACK
I	P-B5!

Black loses no time setting the passed Pawn in motion.

2	K-B1	P-N4
3	P-N4	....

With two Pawns to one on the King-side, White hopes to convert them into a passed Pawn. However, this proves to be much too slow.

3	....	K-N3
4	R-KB7	P-B6
5	K-K1	R-Q1!

By cutting off White's King from further approach to the passed Pawn, Black threatens 6 ... P-B7, winning at once.

6	R-B2	P-N5
7	P-KR4	R-Q5
8	R-KN2	K-N4
9	P-R5	P-N6!

Black makes room for the advance of his King.

10	PxP	K-N5
11	P-N5	KxP
12	P-N6	PxP
13	RxP	P-B7
14	R-N6ch	K-R6
15	R-R6ch	K-N5
16	R-QN6ch	K-B4
	Resigns	

White has run out of checks. Now the Bishop Pawn must queen.

In Diagram 189, too, the winner's superior force will consist of a passed Pawn. But here the passed Pawn will be created. Another point of resemblance to the previous example is that the winner's King plays a very important role.

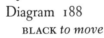

WHITE	BLACK
1 P-B5!!	. . . .

In Diagram 189 the Pawn position is blocked, and it is not clear how White can make progress. Yet with this stroke the whole situation changes radically. White opens up a line of in-

Diagram 188
BLACK *to move*

WHITE
Black wins

Diagram 189
BLACK

WHITE *to move*
White wins

vasion for his King and, equally important, creates a formidable passed King Pawn.

1	. ....	PxP
2	K-B4	R-K3

There is no point in trying to defend the Pawn with 2 ... K-N3, as White simply drives the King off with 3 R-KN3ch.

3	KxP	....

If Black wants to prevent the advance of the powerful King Pawn the logical reply is 3 ... K-B2. But this would lead to 4 R-KN3, R-K1; 5 R-N6 (threatens R-R6), R-KR1; 6 P-K6ch, K-B1; 7 K-K5 followed by K-Q6; and Black would be smothered.

3	....	R-N3

This has the merit of preventing White's Rook from occupying the King Knight file. On the other hand, the terrible King Pawn is now free to advance.

4	P-K6	R-N5
5	K-K5	....

Now Black can try to fight for control of the queening·square, but to no avail: 5 ... K-B1; 6 K-Q6, K-K1; 7 R-KB3, R-N2 (if Black plays 7 ... RxQP or ... RxRP, then White wins on the spot with 8 P-K7); 8 R-B5, R-R2; 9 R-N5 (threatening R-N8 mate), R-R1; 10 R-N7—and White wins quickly.

5	....	R-K5ch
6	K-Q6	RxQP

Or 6 ... K-B1; 7 K-Q7 followed by 8 R-KB3ch and 9 P-K7, etc.

7	R-K3!	Resigns

Black realizes that the situation is hopeless. For example: 7 ...
R-K5; 8 RxR, PxR; 9 P-K7, K-B2; 10 K-Q7; and the Pawn
queens. Another possibility: 7 ... K-B1; 8 P-K7ch, K-K1; 9 R-
KB3; and 10 R-B8 mate.

ROOK AGAINST MINOR PIECE

We know from the table of relative values that a Rook is stronger
than a Bishop or Knight. This strength factor is expressed in
superior mobility. In Diagram 190 the power of Black's Rook is
felt from the start, even though the Rook does not make a move
for the first eleven moves. Black sets his King-side Pawn majority
in motion with the idea of converting it into a passed Pawn. The
Black King takes up an aggressive position, and in due course the
Black Rook delivers a series of smashing blows. Here is Black's
winning procedure as pictured in Diagram 190:

	WHITE	BLACK
1	....	K-K2
2	B-N5	P-B4
3	K-K3	K-B3
4	P-QR4	K-K4

Black's King is now poised for invasion. But first his King-side
Pawns must take a more aggressive stance.

5	P-B3	P-QR4
6	B-B6	P-KN4!
7	P-R3	P-R4
8	B-B3	P-N5
9	PxP	RPxP
10	B-K2	P-KB5ch!

This confronts White with an ugly choice: if 11 K-Q2, P-B6!;
12 PxP, P-N6!; 13 B-B1, K-B5!; 14 B-N2, R-KR1!; 15 K-K2,
R-R7; 16 K-B1, K-K6; and White is helpless.

11	K-B2	K-B4

Diagram 190
BLACK *to move*

WHITE
Black wins

Diagram 191
BLACK *to move*

WHITE
Black wins

	12	B-B1	R-K1!

At last the Rook comes into action—and very effectively, too.

	13	B-K2	P-N6ch!

If now 14 K-K1, P-B6!; 15 PxP, P-N7; 16 K-B2, RxBch!; 17 KxR, P-N8/Q; and Black wins.

14	K-B1	R-K6
15	B-Q1	K-K4

The simplest solution, although Black can also go in for 15 ... RxP!; 16 B-B2, P-B5; 17 K-K2, P-B6ch!; 18 PxP, K-B5!; 19 BxR, PxBch and Black forces the queening of a Pawn.

16	B-B2	P-B6!

At last Black gets his passed Pawn.

17	PxP	RxBPch
18	K-N1	R-B7
	Resigns	

Black wins some Pawns, while White's game remains hopeless.

In Diagram 191 the Bishop and three Pawns are stronger than the Rook, but it takes very fine play to demonstrate this proposition. White's King is tied to its present area by Black's Queen Knight Pawn, but Black needs an additional threat on the Kingside. To establish such a menace he sacrifices two Pawns.

	WHITE	BLACK
1	....	P-N5!
2	PxP	P-B5!

This is the passed Pawn that will win the game.

3	P-N5	B-Q5!
4	R-Q1	B-K6!
5	KxP	B-B8!

Threatening ... P-N8/Q.

6	R-Q6ch	KxP
7	R-QN6	P-B6
8	K-Q3	....

White wants to have his King in position to stop the Bishop Pawn from queening. But Black foils him.

8	....	K-B5
9	R-N8	K-N6
10	R-N8ch	K-B7

Black's King blocks the further advance of his Bishop Pawn, but this is only temporary. The main thing is that one of White's pieces must now backtrack to prevent the Knight Pawn from queening.

11	K-B2	K-K7
12	R-K8ch	K-B8

13	R-KB8	P-B7
14	R-B7	K-K7
15	R-K7ch	K-B6!
16	R-KB7ch	B-B5!
	Resigns	

Black's Bishop Pawn must queen.

ENDINGS WITH A PIECE AHEAD

In endgames where one of the players is a piece ahead, he usually has an easy win. There are, however, some exceptions to the rule that superior force wins, and these exceptions are worth knowing.

In Diagram 176 we noticed a peculiarity of the Rook Pawn in King and Pawn endings which makes a draw possible for the weaker side. In Diagrams 192 and 193 we find another example of the Rook Pawn's propensity to create a draw.

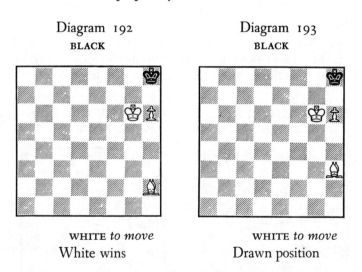

Diagram 192	Diagram 193
BLACK	**BLACK**
WHITE *to move*	**WHITE** *to move*
White wins	Drawn position

Diagram 192 is a straightforward win for the stronger side. Note that the Pawn's queening square is on the same color as the squares on which the Bishop travels. This enables the stronger side to win with ease:

WHITE	BLACK
1 B-K5ch	K-N1
2 P-R7ch	K-B1
3 P-R8/Qch and wins	

In Diagram 193 we encounter a slight but subtle difference. Here the queening square is of the "wrong color." The Bishop travels on white squares, the queening square is a black square. Because of this difference, White cannot win.

If he plays 1 B-K6 or 1 P-R7, Black is immediately stalemated. Other attempts prove equally unsuccessful; for example:

WHITE	BLACK
1 K-R5	K-R2
2 B-B5ch	K-R1
3 K-N6	K-N1
4 P-R7ch	K-R1

And once more Black will be stalemated.

The ending Rook and Bishop against Rook can be won only when the weaker side's King has been driven all the way back. Diagram 194 offers a fine example of the winning technique.

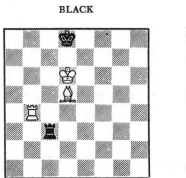

Diagram 194
BLACK

WHITE *to move*
White wins

Diagram 195
BLACK

WHITE *to move*
Drawn position

WHITE	BLACK
1 B-B4!	....

The immediate 1 R-N8ch would, of course, have been answered by 1 ... R-B1. But now interposition is impossible, and in addition Black's Rook has no annoying checks.

1	....	K-B1
2	B-K6ch	K-Q1
3	R-N8ch	R-B1
4	RxR mate	

In Diagram 195 our old friend the Rook Pawn again demonstrates his power to force a draw. Incredible as it may seem, there are exceptional situations in which a Queen cannot win against a Pawn. In Diagram 195 Black is threatening to queen his Pawn. If White plays 1 Q-KN3ch, Black replies 1 ... K-R8, putting himself in a stalemate position. If White then moves his Queen off the King Knight file—in order to lift the stalemate possibility—then Black plays his King out again, threatening to queen his Pawn. White can make no headway, for each time the Black King is driven into the corner, the stalemate threat again arises.

Curiously enough, there are situations in which the Bishop Pawn can force a draw against a Queen. Diagram 196 demonstrates such a position.

WHITE	BLACK
1 Q-N3ch	....

As in the play from Diagram 179, White expects to force 1 ... K-B8. This would block the passed Pawn and give White's King time to approach for the ultimate checkmate. But Black has a fine resource:

1	....	K-R8!

This is the move that saves Black, for 2 QxP stalemates him.

Meanwhile, he is threatening to queen his Pawn, and White has no useful checks. For example:

2	Q-KR3ch	K-N8
3	Q-KN3ch	K-R8!

Obviously White can make no headway. The game is a draw.

Diagram 196	Diagram 197
BLACK	BLACK

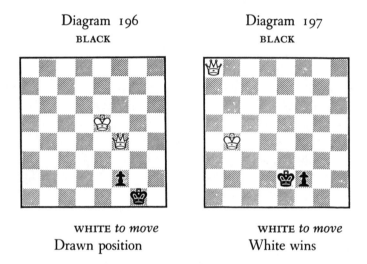

WHITE *to move*	WHITE *to move*
Drawn position	White wins

Diagram 197 shows an exceptional position in which the Bishop Pawn loses against the Queen. This is due to the fact that the White King is near enough for the kill:

	WHITE·	BLACK
1	Q-N2!	K-K8
2	K-B3!	P-B8/Q
3	Q-Q2 mate!	

The few exceptions which conclude this chapter should not blind us to the general rule that *superior force wins*. In the vast majority of cases this holds true, and it is the very essence of good chess play to be able to exploit a material advantage.

EIGHTH REVIEW TEST
(answers on pages 137–138)

1. The endgame is the stage at which a ＿＿＿＿＿＿＿＿ advantage tells.
2. The ＿＿＿＿＿＿＿, which in the early stages had to be carefully guarded and shielded, now becomes a powerful unit.
3. A player who is a Pawn ahead is potentially a ＿＿＿＿＿＿ ahead.
4. [Diagram 170] White (can/cannot) force checkmate.
5. [Diagram 171] White (can/cannot) force checkmate.
6. [Diagram 171] White has a Pawn which can be converted into a ＿＿＿＿＿＿; he must therefore win.
7. The two Kings are in ＿＿＿＿＿＿ when they face each other on the same line, separated by an odd number of squares.
8. The Opposition on a ＿＿＿＿＿＿ is by far the most important.
9. The player whose King (does/does not) have to move is said to have the Opposition.
10. The player with the extra Pawn will (win/draw) if he has the Opposition after his Pawn has advanced to the sixth rank.
11. In the basic ending of King and Pawn against King, if the Pawn gives check on advancing to the seventh rank, the position is a (win/draw).
12. [Diagram 173] After 2 P-K6??, K-Q1; 3 P-K7ch; Black plays 3 ... ＿＿＿＿＿＿ forcing 4 ＿＿＿＿＿＿ in reply. At this point Black (draws/loses) by ＿＿＿＿＿＿.
13. [Diagram 175] After 11 P-K7ch, we know the position is a (win/draw) because the Pawn gives check while advancing to the sixth rank.
14. [Diagram 176] White can (win/draw) with 4 K-N5.
15. [Diagram 177] After 4 ... P-N8/Q, Black threatens to win with 5 ... ＿＿＿＿＿＿ or 5 ... ＿＿＿＿＿＿.
16. [Diagram 178] After 2 ... K-B3; 3 K-K5; White queens (one move/two moves) ahead of Black.

17. A passed Pawn is one whose advance is not hampered by hostile Pawns on neighboring _____.

18. [Diagram 180] If Black moves first, his King (can/cannot) stop White's outside passed Pawn.

19. [Diagram 181] White can also win by starting with 1 _____.

20. [Diagram 182] After 1 . . . P-B6!; 2 NxP, BxN; 3 PxB, K-B5; 4 K-Q2, K-N6; 5 K-Q3, KxP; there could follow 6 P-B4, K-N5; 7 K-Q4; and Black would win after 7 . . . _____; 8 _____, _____; 9 _____, _____; 10 _____, _____; etc.

21. [Diagram 182] If White plays 12 K-B1, Black wins with 12 . . . _____.

22. [Diagram 182] After 15 K-R2, K-Q6; 16 KxP, KxP; 17 K-N3; Black has the winning reply 17 . . . _____.

23. [Diagram 183] If White plays 12 PxP, Black wins a piece with 12 . . . _____.

24. [Diagram 183] After 21 P-N4, RPxPch; 22 PxP, PxPch; 23 KxP; the race to queen a Pawn is won by (White/Black). Reason?

25. [Diagram 183] After 24 . . . P-R7, White resigns because he cannot prevent 25 . . . _____.

26. [Diagram 184] If White plays 2 PxP, Black replies 2 . . . _____ and then captures White's _____ _____.

27. [Diagram 184] After playing 6 . . . N-N6, Black threatens 7 . . . NxB; 8 KxN, K-B6—with a view to 9 . . . _____.

28. [Diagram 184] Black plays 12 . . . N-B8ch! in order to force White's King away from Queen 2, making it possible for Black to play . . . _____.

29. [Diagram 184] White must play his King to the King-side on move 13 because Black is threatening to play 13 . . . _____.

30. [Diagram 185] Black plays 7 . . . B-N3 in order to defend his _____.

31. [Diagram 185] White plays 11 P-R5! in order to prevent Black from playing . . . _____.

32. [Diagram 185] When White plays 15 P-R6, he threatens to win a piece with 16 _____.

33. [Diagram 185] Black (can/cannot) defend himself against this threat.

34. [Diagram 187] White can also win with 1 _____.

35. [Diagram 188] If White plays 6 RxP, Black wins with 6 . . . _____.

36. [Diagram 188] If White plays 13 PxP, Black wins with 13 . . . _____.

37. [Diagram 188] If White plays 16 R-R1, Black's quickest winning move is 16 . . . _____.

38. [Diagram 189] With 1 P-B5!! White threatens 2 _____ and wins.

39. [Diagram 189] If Black plays 3 . . . K-B2 and White replies 4 R-KN3, White is threatening to win with 5 _____. Reason?

40. [Diagram 190] If White answers 13 . . . P-N6ch! with 14 K-B3, Black replies 14 . . . _____.

41. [Diagram 191] If Black plays 3 . . . BxP, White replies 4 _____ followed by 5 _____.

42. [Diagram 194] If Black plays 1 . . . K-K1, White replies 2 _____.

43. [Diagram 197] If Black plays 2 . . . P-B8/N, White replies 3 _____, and Black is helpless.

Eighth Review Test: Answers

1. Pawn
2. King
3. Queen
4. cannot
5. can
6. Queen
7. Opposition
8. file
9. does not
10. win
11. draw
12. K-K1; K-K6; draws; stalemate
13. draw
14. draw
15. Q-N7ch; Q-KR8ch

16. two
17. files
18. can
19. K-B5
20. P-R5; P-B5, P-R6; P-B6, P-R7; P-B7, P-R8/Qch
21. P-R7
22. K-B6
23. BxPch
24. Black; there follows 23 ... P-N6; 24 PxP, PxP; 25 P-B5, P-N7; 26 P-B6, P-N8/Q; 27 P-B7, Q-N3ch and wins
25. P-R8/Q
26. KxP; Queen Pawn
27. KxP
28. K-B6

29. N-K6
30. Pawn at Queen Bishop 4
31. ... B-N3
32. P-R7
33. cannot
34. R-KN8
35. P-B7
36. P-B7
37. K-N6
38. P-B6ch
39. R-N7ch; after 5 R-N7ch, KxR; 6 KxR; White's King Pawn must queen
40. R-K6 mate
41. KxP; KxP
42. R-B8 mate
43. K-Q3

CHAPTER 6

PRINCIPLES OF OPENING PLAY

IN THE preceding chapters we have seen how the chessmen operate—how they attack, defend, threaten, win material, give checkmate. Now we come to the crucial question, "How do we put them in position to be effective?" In other words, how do we get them to unfold their maximum power to menace the enemy forces and protect their own?

In the opening position (Diagram 2) the pieces are all on the back row. There they are utterly useless, as they can function powerfully only when they have moved up for action. (It is true that the King should not get into the thick of the fight, but we need to castle if we are to give the King the maximum amount of protection. And we cannot castle until we have moved the King Knight and King Bishop out of the way.)

So, to begin with, we must "develop" the pieces, get them off their original squares, and place them where they may be used aggressively. It will be helpful to learn a few basic principles to guide us in our opening play.

ALWAYS PLAY 1 P-K4

To the beginner the choice of an opening move is a complete mystery. He has no precept or maxim to go by; he has no theory to rely on. It helps him enormously to narrow down the choice to a single move. That move, for our purposes, is 1 P-K4.

We have two reasons for making this choice. In the first place we can realize very quickly that pieces are generally placed most effectively in the center sector of the board, for from this area their power radiates to all parts of the board. However, a Pawn placed securely in the center controls certain center squares. This means that hostile pieces cannot move to the controlled squares, since after doing so, they would be captured.

In Diagram 198, for example, Black cannot play 1 ... N-Q4? because of the reply 2 PxN. He can't play 1 ... B-B4? because of the reply 2 PxB.

<table>
<tr><td align="center">Diagram 198
BLACK to move</td><td align="center">Diagram 199
BLACK to move</td></tr>
<tr><td align="center">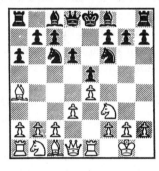</td><td align="center"></td></tr>
<tr><td align="center">WHITE
Black must not play ...
N-Q4? or ... B-B4?</td><td align="center">WHITE
Black must not play ...
N-Q4?</td></tr>
</table>

In Diagram 199 Black's Knight at Queen Knight 3 is rather out of play. It would be desirable to bring the Knight to the center of the board, but ... N-Q4 is out of the question, as White would simply reply PxN. Thus, we see that White's Pawn control of the important Queen 5 square keeps Black's Knight out of play.

Another point about 1 P-K4 is that it opens lines for White's King Bishop and his Queen. As we shall see later on, it is not desirable to move the Queen out early in the game. On the other hand, it is important to play out the King Bishop fairly quickly, partly for attacking purposes and partly to prepare for castling.

Another good way to start the game—on the principle of beginning with a move of a center Pawn—is to play 1 P-Q4. But as this leads to complicated and subtle play, we recommend 1 P-K4 as simpler and safer.

DEVELOP YOUR PIECES

As we have seen, the pieces are useless on the back line. Only when they have been developed can they function actively for attack and defense. If both players develop equally efficiently, the prospects will be more or less even. Such a situation is shown in Diagram 200. Both players have brought out a Knight and a Bishop. In fact, White, having developed his King Knight, is ready to move his King to safety by castling.

Diagram 200

BLACK

WHITE *to move*

Both players have developed sensibly

Diagram 201

BLACK

WHITE *to move*

White has a good development; Black, a bad one

Diagram 201 shows a position that was reached by the following moves:

WHITE   BLACK
1   P-K4   . . . .

White begins with the recommended move.

1   . . . .   P-Q3

But Black courts trouble with a move that may lead to a cramped, lifeless position. His best is 1 . . . P-K4.

2   P-Q4   . . . .

When both center Pawns are abreast on the fourth rank, the position is known as a "broad center." White has opened the diagonals for both Bishops. His two formidable center Pawns control the center. Since the prospects for bringing out Black's pieces are not good, he seems headed for trouble.

2   . . . .   P-QB3?

Not good. Black fails to make a developing move, such as 2 . . . N-KB3, or one disputing White's command of the center.

Another drawback in Black's last move is that it makes . . . N-QB3 impossible. Thus, Black is deprived of a good developing move.

3   N-KB3   . . . .

Excellent. Having taken a commanding position with his center Pawns, White now develops his King Knight effectively. Because Knights are short-stepping pieces, they should be developed in or near the center. For example, when played to King Bishop 3, this Knight bears down on the King 5 and Queen 4 squares, located in the heart of the center. By the same reasoning, such moves as N-K2 or N-R3 would be vastly inferior.

3   . . . .   P-B3?

Another very bad move. Black keeps on making Pawn moves and neglects the development of his pieces. ... P-B3, in addition, deprives Black's King Knight of his best square. There is still one further drawback: Black weakens a vital diagonal leading right to his King.

4   B-QB4   ....

White places his finger on the weakness. The Bishop here has a magnificent diagonal leading right into the enemy camp.

4   ....   N-KR3

A Knight is almost always badly placed at the side of the board, but Black has no choice. The best square for this Knight would have been King Bishop 3, giving the Knight an important role in the center; but since 3 ... P-B3? has deprived the Knight of this good square, Black has no choice.

5   Castles   ....

White is making splendid progress. He controls the center, he has two pieces developed, he has brought his King to a safe position.

As for Black, he has made three wasteful (or harmful) Pawn moves and developed only one piece, badly at that.

5   ....   N-B2

Black brings his Knight nearer to the center zone and also closes the diagonal so that he can castle after developing his King Bishop. But now Black has made *two* moves to get his Knight to an inferior square.

6   N-B3   ....

Bringing out another piece, White further increases his lead.

6 ....   P-K4

Finally, and under most disadvantageous circumstances, Black makes the Pawn move that should have been his first move.

7 B-K3   ....

White steadily continues his development, remaining with much the freer position.

7 ....   B-K2

See Diagram 201. Our verdict is: Black is far behind in development, his pieces have very little scope, his whole Queen-side remains undeveloped, his prospects for the rest of the game are meager. Clearly White has the more promising position, and unless he blunders badly, he should win the game.

AVOID SELF-BLOCKING MOVES

Quick development is a virtue, but only if it is combined with *effective* development. When a player selects moves that cut down the mobility of his pieces, he is laying the groundwork for a constricted position that will leave him with very poor prospects during the later play.

Consider, for example, the position shown in Diagram 202, which arises after the moves 1 P-K4, P-K4; 2 N-K2?

The Knight move is very bad, as it blocks the development of White's King Bishop. In addition, at King 2 the Knight is much less effective than he would be at King Bishop 3.

In Diagram 203 we see the consequences of a somewhat related mistake after the moves 1 P-K4, P-K4; 2 P-KB3?, B-B4!

With 2 P-KB3? White deprives his King Knight of his best square. In addition he allows Black's King Bishop to take a magnificent diagonal. White is going to have serious trouble in trying to castle (after finally developing his King Bishop and King Knight) because, thanks to his faulty 2 P-KB3?, Black's Bishop at Queen Bishop 4 is aimed directly at the square White's King would have to occupy in castling. It turns out, then, that 2 P-KB3? is a serious mistake that may well cripple White's position for the rest of the game.

Diagram 202

BLACK *to move*

WHITE

White's Knight at King 2 blocks the development of his King Bishop

Diagram 203

BLACK

WHITE *to move*

White's 2 P-KB3? has spoiled his development and given Black's Bishop a splendid diagonal

The position shown in Diagram 204 has been reached after the moves 1 P-K4, P-K4; 2 P-Q3? Here White has voluntarily blocked the development of his King Bishop, which will now remain trapped inside a wall of White Pawns. In doing so, White has condemned himself to a passive, unpromising position.

On the other hand, Black commits a similar mistake in Diagram 205. After 1 P-K4, P-K4; 2 N-KB3; he defends his King Pawn with 2 ... B-Q3? This serves the immediate purpose of defense—but short-sightedly, thoughtlessly, and very badly. For what happens? The Bishop at Queen 3 blocks Black's Queen Pawn, which in turn means that Black cannot develop his Queen Bishop. Either this Bishop will have to remain at home indefinitely, or else the Bishop now at Queen 3 will have to be shifted around in some way to allow Black to advance his Queen Pawn.

Diagram 204   Diagram 205
BLACK *to move*   BLACK

WHITE   WHITE *to move*

White has blocked his de-   Black has blocked his development with 2 P-Q3?   velopment with 2 ... B-Q3?

But all this sounds cumbersome and time-consuming, and indeed it is. Whether Black will ever be able to regain the lost ground is very doubtful.

Another self-blocking move is seen in Diagram 206. This arises after 1 P-K4, P-K4; 2 N-KB3, N-QB3; 3 P-B3. With his last move White proposes to build a powerful Pawn center by means of P-Q4. But he forgets that by playing 3 P-B3 he is pre-empting the Queen Bishop 3 square, so that a later N-QB3 is impossible.

Black jumps alertly on this point by playing 3 ... P-Q4! Then, after 4 PxP, QxP, Black's Queen takes up a commanding position in the center from which she cannot be dislodged by N-B3 because White has already played P-B3, depriving his Queen Knight of access to the important square. The paradoxical feature of 3 P-B3, then, is that instead of giving White a strong position in the center it gives *Black* a strong position in the center.

After the moves 1 P-K4, P-K4; 2 B-K2, N-KB3; we get the position shown in Diagram 207. The move 2 B-K2 is feeble and unnecessarily self-limiting, and Black immediately seizes the initiative with 2 ... N-KB3, attacking White's King Pawn. If White protects the Pawn with 3 N-QB3 (a developing move),

Diagram 206

BLACK *to move*

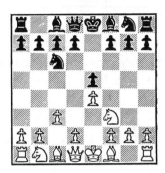

WHITE

White's 3 P-B3 has deprived his Queen Knight of its best square

Diagram 207

BLACK

WHITE *to move*

White's self-limiting 2 B-K2 has allowed Black to seize the initiative

Black replies 3 ... B-N5, threatening to exchange his Bishop for the protective Knight and then capture White's King Pawn. This will probably induce White to play 4 P-Q3 in order to give his King Pawn firm protection. But after 4 P-Q3, White has hemmed in his Bishop and remains enmeshed in a sadly constricted position. From this we see the effects of ceding the initiative with 2 B-K2.

GUARD THE KING

Good development will never endanger your King. Bad development, in addition to its other defects, will often expose your King to fatal attack.

Bad development, by losing time or by unwittingly opening up lines for the enemy pieces, may leave your King helpless against concentrated enemy attack. And bad development, by definition, will deprive you of the resources needed to fight back to protect your King from disaster. The following short games show some of the possible dangers:

BUDAPEST DEFENSE

WHITE	BLACK
1 P-Q4	. . . .

While this move is perfectly playable, you will recall that 1 P-K4 has been recommended as the best move for an inexperienced player.

| | 1   . . . . | N-KB3 |

Here 1 . . . P-Q4 is the conservative reply. But Black is playing for complications.

| | 2 P-QB4 | . . . . |

White has his reasons for controlling the Queen 5 square. He is relying on 2 . . . P-Q4, which he will answer with 3 PxP. Then, after 3 . . . NxP, he will play 4 P-K4, obtaining a broad Pawn center, while after 3 . . . QxP, he will gain time attacking the Queen with 4 N-QB3.

But Black has plans of his own.

| | 2   . . . . | P-K4!? |

A very complicated idea. After 3 PxP, N-N5, White runs the danger of losing valuable time by trying to hold on to the offered Pawn See Diagram 208.

However, by playing 3 PxP, N-N5; 4 B-B4, N-QB3; 5 N-KB3; White could further his development nicely and hold on to the Pawn for a while, at any rate.

| | 3 P-Q5? | . . . . |

But this is a sheer waste of time. Besides, it gives Black a fine square for his King Bishop.

3 ....   B-B4!

Black loses no time in taking advantage of the opportunity offered him. Note that he has two pieces developed, while White

Diagram 208	Diagram 209
BLACK	**BLACK**

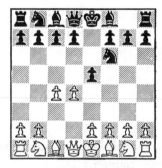

WHITE *to move*	WHITE
After 2 ... P-K4!?	White is checkmated

has no piece in action. This is a sure indication that White is on the wrong track.

4   B-N5??   ....

At last a developing move, but the wrong kind. White should have tried 4 N-KB3.

4 ....   N-K5!!

Black alertly offers his Queen.

5   BxQ   BxP mate!

See Diagram 209. This is a classic example of the way in which backward development can endanger one's King.

Here is another example of what happens when the King's safety is neglected:

CARO-KANN DEFENSE

WHITE	BLACK
1 P-K4	P-QB3

This is a departure from the more customary 1 ... P-K4. The advance of the Queen Bishop Pawn does not contribute to Black's development; it does, however, initiate a plan to dispute White's contemplated control of the center.

2 P-Q4	....

White establishes a broad Pawn center. If Black is not to be smothered, he must immediately adopt counteraction:

2	P-Q4

Good. Black takes a solid position in the center and at the same time threatens ... PxP. After 3 PxP, PxP Black would have a perfectly secure position in the center. The same would be true of 3 P-K5, B-B4.

3 B-Q3?!	....

White guards his King Pawn with a developing move which is, however, of questionable value. (Generally speaking, it is better to play out Knights before Bishops in the opening. The reason for this is that the Knights, with their limited mobility, have no great choice of the best developing moves. The Bishops, on the other hand, have greater mobility, but at this point in the game it is not clear which square will turn out to be the most effective.)

A better move than the one actually played by White, then, would have been 3 N-QB3.

See Diagram 210.

3	....	N-KB3?

A serious waste of time, as the Knight will at once be driven back. The right way was 3 ... PxP!; 4 BxP, N-B3. This would have allowed Black to gain time to develop by attacking the Bishop.

4	P-K5!	KN-Q2

Now Black's pieces are ineffectually crowded together with no hope of achieving freedom.

5	P-K6!	....

To this there is no better reply than 5 ... N-B3, although Black would be badly off after 6 PxPch, KxP, etc.

5	....	PxP??

Black snatches the Pawn, not realizing what White has in mind. Note that he has now uncovered a vital diagonal leading

Diagram 210
BLACK *to move*

WHITE

Black must now choose between good development and bad development

Diagram 211
BLACK

WHITE

Black is checkmated

to his King. This is the consequence of Black's botched development.

6   Q-R5ch!   . . . .

White immediately exploits the opening. Black's reply is forced.

6   . . . .   P-KN3
7   QxNPch!   . . . .

Black's mistake is so gross that White can win by sacrificing his Queen.

7   . . . .   PxQ
8   BxP mate

See Diagram 211.

So much for the principles underlying good opening play. In the next chapter we shall try to apply these principles to some of the more common chess openings.

NINTH REVIEW TEST
(answers on pages 154–155)

1. [Diagram 2] When the pieces are still on the _____ rank, they are utterly useless.
2. The process of getting the pieces off their original squares is known as _____ them.
3. Pieces are generally placed most effectively in the _____ of the board.
4. This is because from this area their power _____ to all parts of the board.
5. A Pawn placed in the center controls vital _____.

6. This means that hostile pieces cannot move to the _____ squares.
7. [Diagram 198] Black cannot play ... N-Q5, because the Knight is _____ by White's Bishop at Queen Rook 4.
8. [Diagram 199] Black (should/should not) play ... NxP.
9. [Diagram 199] If Black plays ... NxP, White replies _____ or _____.
10. The move 1 P-K4 opens lines for White's _____ _____ and his _____.
11. It is not desirable to move out the _____ early in the game.
12. One of the reasons for playing out the King Bishop early in the game is to prepare for _____.
13. The best way to start the game is to advance a _____ Pawn.
14. Only when the pieces have been developed can they function actively for attack and _____.
15. [Diagram 200] White (is/is not) ready to castle.
16. Because Knights are short-stepping pieces, they should be developed in or near the _____.
17. It is almost always bad play to place a _____ at the side of the board.
18. [Diagram 201] (White/Black) has much more freedom of action.
19. [Diagram 202] White's King Knight (would/would not) be much more effective at King Bishop 3.
20. [Diagram 203] 2 P-KB3? is a bad move because it prevents White from playing _____.
21. [Diagram 203] White will have trouble trying to castle later in the game because of the commanding position of Black's _____.
22. [Diagram 204] White has blocked the development of his _____ _____ by playing 2 P-Q3?
23. [Diagram 205] Black has blocked the advance of his _____ _____ by playing 2 ... B-Q3?

24. [Diagram 205] As a result of 2 ... B-Q3? Black will be unable to develop his _____ _____.
25. [Diagram 206] White has played 3 P-B3 in order to build a broad _____ center.
26. [Diagram 206] By playing P-B3, White has made it impossible for him to play _____.
27. [Diagram 207] Black threatens ... _____.
28. Bad development will often expose your _____ to fatal attack.
29. [Diagram 208] 3 P-Q5? is feeble because it gives Black a fine square for his _____ _____.
30. [Diagram 208] After 3 P-Q5?, B-B4, (White/Black) is ahead in development.
31. [Diagram 208] After 3 P-Q5, B-B4; 4 B-N5??; Black can win a Pawn with 4 ... _____; 5 _____, _____ or _____.
32. [Diagram 209] White (can/cannot) play K-Q2.
33. Generally speaking, it is better to play out _____ before _____ in the opening.
34. [Diagram 210] After 3 ... N-KB3?; 4 P-K5!; Black cannot play 4 ... N-K5? because White replies 5 _____, winning a piece.
35. [Diagram 210] After 3 ... N-KB3?; 4 P-K5!, KN-Q2; 5 P-K6!, PxP??; 6 Q-R5ch!, P-KN3; White can also force mate with 7 _____, _____; 8 _____.
36. [Diagram 211] Black (can/cannot) play 8 ... K-B2.

Ninth Review Test: Answers

1. first	7. pinned
2. developing	8. should not
3. center	9. BxN; Q-R4ch and QxN
4. radiates	10. King Bishop; Queen
5. squares	11. Queen
6. controlled	12. castling

13. center
14. defense
15. is
16. center
17. Knight
18. White
19. would
20. N-KB3
21. Bishop at Queen Bishop 4
22. King Bishop
23. Queen Pawn
24. Queen Bishop
25. Pawn
26. N-B3
27. NxP
28. King
29. King Bishop (at Queen Bishop 4)
30. Black
31. BxPch; KxB, N-K5ch or ... N-N5ch
32. cannot
33. Knights; Bishops
34. P-KB3
35. BxPch, PxB; QxNP mate
36. cannot

CHAPTER 7

SOME MODEL OPENINGS

WE MAY define an opening as a standardized pattern of beginning moves. Each opening has its special name. In some cases the very first move made by White or Black gives the opening its name. In other cases a number of specific moves have to be made before the opening has the identification that differentiates it from all other openings.

In some instances an opening is named for the pieces or Pawns that play the salient role. This is true, for example, of the Four Knights' Game in which all four Knights are developed very rapidly.

On the other hand, there are cases where an opening is named for the player or occasion which first popularized it. This is true of the English Opening (1 P-QB4), first used extensively by the Englishman Staunton in his match against the French master St. Amant in 1843.

The openings have all been subjected to very detailed analysis with extensive discussion of alternative possibilities. To the inexperienced player most of this voluminous material is useless, partly because so much of it depends on memorizing and partly because the opponent can render so much of it useless by varying from the accepted lines of play.

In this chapter we shall, therefore, devote our attention to some of the ideas that underlie standard openings. If we can grasp the basic idea, we can often get a reliable notion of the kind of play that will later take place in the middle game. We shall deal here only with openings in which White begins with 1 P-K4 and Black replies 1 ... P-K4.

In most of these openings the main strategical problem revolves about White's hope of securing an advantage in the center by playing P-Q4. But, as we shall see, the earlier White plays this move, the less likely he is to secure any advantage.

CENTER GAME

Here White plays P-Q4 at the earliest possible moment and, as a result, allows the initiative to slip through his hands.

WHITE	BLACK
1 P-K4	P-K4
2 P-Q4	....

This advance requires some preparation, at least with N-KB3.

2	PxP
3 QxP	....

At first sight it seems that White has given his Queen a commanding position in the center, but it is almost always a mistake to develop the Queen early in the game. This premature development exposes the Queen to attack by hostile pieces.

3	N-QB3!

Black immediately exploits the early development of White's Queen by attacking her, thus gaining time. See Diagram 212.

4 Q-K3	N-B3

Black continues the policy of rapid development.

	5	N-QB3	B-N5
	6	B-Q2	Castles
	7	Castles	R-K1!

Black has a considerable lead in development and threatens to win a Pawn by ... BxN, etc., undermining White's King Pawn. See Diagram 213.

<table>
<tr><td>Diagram 212</td><td>Diagram 213</td></tr>
<tr><td>BLACK</td><td>BLACK</td></tr>
</table>

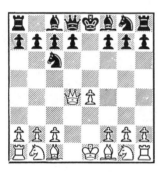

WHITE *to move*	WHITE *to move*
White has lost valuable time with the premature development of his Queen	Black threatens to win a Pawn. In any event his development remains superior

DANISH GAMBIT

A gambit is an opening in which a player sacrifices material, generally a Pawn, in the hope of securing a compensating advantage, usually a notable lead in development.

WHITE		BLACK
1	P-K4	P-K4
2	P-Q4	PxP
3	P-QB3	....

This is the gambit. Instead of recapturing (3 QxP), White plays for rapid development.

3	....	PxP
4	B-QB4	PxP
5	BxNP	....

See Diagram 214. It must be admitted that the White Bishops look menacing, but two Pawns are a great deal to part with; it remains to be seen whether White's lead in development is worth two Pawns.

5	....	P-QB3

Black carefully sets up a hedgehog position to make himself unassailable. The purpose of his last move is to prevent White from occupying the important Queen 5 square. In addition, Black may find it useful to play ... P-QN4 or ... P-Q4 at the right moment.

6	N-QB3	....

Against 6 Q-N3 (which looks strong), Black has a good reply in 6 ... Q-K2! defending the King Bishop Pawn and also threatening 7 ... P-Q4, or even better 7 ... Q-N5ch which would destroy White's attacking chances altogether.

6	....	P-Q3

Black is in no hurry to play the natural developing move 6 ... N-KB3, as the Knight would merely be driven back with 7 P-K5.

By first playing 6 ... P-Q3, Black neutralizes the advance of White's King Pawn and also paves the way for his next move.

7	N-B3	N-Q2!

The beginning of an interesting maneuver. As Black's position is solid, he can afford to put up with a somewhat cramped position.

8	Castles	N-B4!

See Diagram 215. Now Black is ready to play . . . B-K3, either eliminating White's King Bishop or inducing its withdrawal from its best square. Black's backward development does him no harm, since his position has no weak points.

Diagram 214
BLACK *to move*

Diagram 215
BLACK

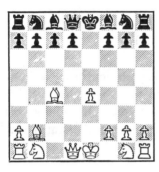

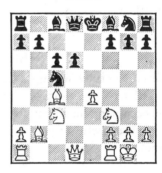

WHITE
White's Bishops look formidable

WHITE *to move*
Black has a solid defensive formation

KING'S GAMBIT

This gambit involves the speculative offer of White's King Bishop Pawn. The offer is made with the hope of removing Black's King Pawn from the center. White's objective is to set up subsequently, a broad Pawn center with P-Q4. In addition, he hopes to secure an attack along the King Bishop file.

WHITE	BLACK
1 P-K4	P-K4
2 P-KB4	PxP
3 N-KB3	. . . .

The immediate 3 P-Q4 would be answered by 3 . . . Q-R5ch —an awkward move to meet. White, therefore, rules out the Queen check with a developing move.

3	....	P-KN4

Black defends his advanced King Bishop Pawn even before it is attacked. Also, he prepares to "fianchetto" his King Bishop— that is, to play it to King Knight 2.

4	P-KR4	....

White breaks up the Black Pawn chain, so as to deprive Black's foremost King Bishop Pawn of Pawn protection.

4	....	P-N5
5	N-K5	....

See Diagram 216. White expects 5 . . . P-KR4 (to protect the King Knight Pawn); 6 B-B4, R-R2; 7 P-Q4, which would leave White with a formidable position.

5	....	N-KB3!

Attacking White's King Pawn.

<table>
<tr><td>Diagram 216</td><td>Diagram 217</td></tr>
<tr><td>BLACK to move</td><td>BLACK</td></tr>
</table>

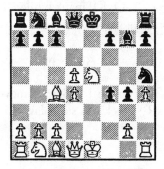

<table>
<tr><td>WHITE</td><td>WHITE to move</td></tr>
</table>

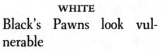

Black's Pawns look vulnerable

Black has a solid position

6   B-B4   . . . .

White counters with an attack against Black's King Bishop
Pawn.

6   . . . .   P-Q4!
7   PxP   B-N2
8   P-Q4   N-R4

Black stands well. This form of the King's Gambit is known as
the Kieseritzky Gambit. See Diagram 217.

KING'S GAMBIT DECLINED

Since the King's Gambit often leads to dangerous complications,
many players prefer to play safe by declining the gambit.

WHITE	BLACK
1 P-K4	P-K4
2 P-KB4	B-B4

See Diagram 218. Black offers a Pawn which apparently
can be taken free of charge. However, if White plays 3 PxP??
Black wins with 3 . . . Q-R5ch. In that case 4 K-K2 is answered
by 4 . . . QxKP mate, while 4 P-KN3 is refuted by 4 . . . QxKPch
and 5 . . . QxR.

3   N-KB3   P-Q3

The reason for Black's move here is that after 4 PxP, PxP; 5
NxP?; Black can still play 5 . . . Q-R5ch, etc.

4   B-B4   N-KB3

Counterattacking against White's King Pawn.

5   N-B3   N-B3

6	P-Q3	B-K3
7	B-N5	P-QR3
8	BxNch	PxB

See Diagram 219. The position is about equal, for after 9 PxP, PxP; 10 NxP?; Black wins a piece with 10 . . . Q-Q5!

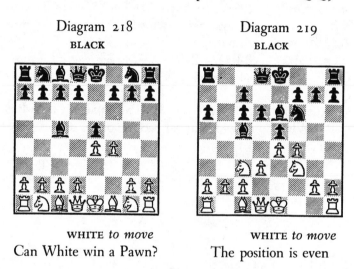

Diagram 218	Diagram 219
BLACK	**BLACK**
WHITE *to move*	**WHITE** *to move*
Can White win a Pawn?	The position is even

PHILIDOR'S DEFENSE

This gives Black a very cramped position and is therefore not recommended.

	WHITE	BLACK
1	P-K4	P-K4
2	N-KB3	P-Q3

Black blocks the diagonal of his King Bishop and condemns himself to a very crowded position.

3	P-Q4	N-Q2

Black does not want to "give up the center" with 3 . . . PxP;

but the move he actually makes accentuates the cramped character of his position.

4   B-QB4!   ....

See Diagram 220.

Black must now play very carefully. For example, if 4 ...
KN-B3; 5 N-N5; and the only way for Black to parry the threat
of 6 NxBP is to give up a Pawn with 5 ... P-Q4.

Note that 4 ... B-K2?; 5 PxP, PxP? is even worse because of
6 Q-Q5! when Black has no really good reply to the threat of
7 QxBP mate.

Another possibility is 4 ... B-K2?; 5 PxP, NxP; 6 NxN, PxN;
7 Q-R5. White must win material because of his double threat:
8 QxBPch or 8 QxKP.

While we have seen that in general it is not good policy to
play out the Queen early, that policy may be used here because
it leads to a tangible gain.

4   ....   P-QB3

Even here White may try a sacrificial attack by 5 PxP, PxP
(if 5 ... NxP; 6 NxN, PxN; 7 BxPch! winning a Pawn, as
Black cannot take the Bishop); 6 BxPch!?, KxB; 7 NxPch (this
Knight cannot be captured). White's attack is very strong, as the
Black King is dangerously exposed.

5	N-B3	B-K2
6	Castles	KN-B3
7	P-QR4	....

This prevents a Queen-side expansion of Black's game by ...
P-QN4, etc.

7	....	Castles
8	Q-K2	....

See Diagram 221.

White's position is much freer and he has an easy, natural development for his pieces. Black's situation, on the other hand,

<table>
<tr><td>Diagram 220</td><td>Diagram 221</td></tr>
<tr><td>BLACK *to move*</td><td>BLACK *to move*</td></tr>
</table>

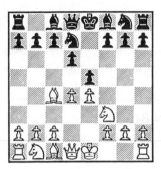 

<table>
<tr><td>WHITE</td><td>WHITE</td></tr>
<tr><td>Black has a poor position in which he can easily go wrong</td><td>White's position is much freer and much more promising</td></tr>
</table>

is constricted, uncomfortable, and unpromising. White undoubtedly has the better prospects for the middle game.

SCOTCH GAME

Once highly popular, this opening is rarely seen nowadays. The initiative is lost fairly quickly by White, though not so blatantly as in the Center Game.

	WHITE	BLACK
1	P-K4	P-K4
2	N-KB3	N-QB3

Black develops a piece to defend his King Pawn; this is far superior to the cramping 2 ... P-Q3 (Philidor's Defense).

3	P-Q4	....

This early advance in the center is the characteristic move of the opening.

    3   ....   PxP
    4   NxP   ....

See Diagram 222.

Material is even, but White has lost time by moving his King Knight twice. This enables Black to take the initiative by developing and gaining time.

    4   ....   N-B3

Black attacks the King Pawn.

    5   N-QB3   ....

White defends.

    5   ....   B-N5

Black pins White's Queen Knight and thereby threatens ... NxP again.

    6   NxN   ....

This exchange is necessary, as White wants to play B-Q3 to protect his King Pawn.

    6   ....   NPxN
    7   B-Q3   P-Q4
    8   PxP   Q-K2ch!

A troublesome move to answer. After 9 B-K2, NxP, White's chances are drawish at best.

    9   Q-K2   NxP

See Diagram 223. A draw is the likely outcome of this rather colorless position.

Diagram 222
BLACK *to move*

WHITE
Black can seize the initiative

Diagram 223
BLACK

WHITE *to move*
The position is approximately even

GIUOCO PIANO

In the variation treated here this is a placid line of play well-suited to inexperienced players. The game develops along sound and inoffensive lines.

WHITE	BLACK
1 P-K4	P-K4
2 N-KB3	N-QB3

As we have noticed earlier, this excellent move enables Black to defend his King Pawn with a developing move.

3 B-B4	B-B4

Both players continue with a policy of sound development.

4 P-Q3 . . . .

White opens the diagonal to develop his Queen Bishop.

> 4   ....   N-B3

Another developing move. Now Black is ready to castle.

> 5   N-B3   P-Q3

The perfectly symmetrical character of this position tells us that neither player has an advantage and that nothing exciting is likely to happen. (See Diagram 224.)

> 6   B-K3   ....

White hopes for 6 ... BxB; 7 PxB; because this will provide him with an open King Bishop file on which his Rooks can operate after he castles.

> 6   ....   B-N3

Black refuses to make the exchange on White's terms. However, he has no objection to White's playing 7 BxB at this point, for after 7 ... RPxB, Black would secure an open Queen Rook file.

> 7   P-KR3   ....

White prefers not to allow the annoying pin by ... B-N5, which could be followed by ... N-Q5 and lead to awkward consequences for White.

> 7   ....   B-K3

Now it is Black who offers the exchange and White who refuses it, for reasons already set forth.

> 8   B-N3   Castles
> 9   Castles   ....

See Diagram 225. An even game, involving little risk for either player.

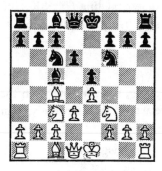

Diagram 224

BLACK

WHITE *to move*

A perfectly symmetrical position

Diagram 225

BLACK *to move*

WHITE

A position with equal chances for both players

FOUR KNIGHTS' GAME

This is another opening which often leads to symmetrical positions ending in a draw.

WHITE	BLACK
1 P-K4	P-K4
2 N-KB3	N-QB3
3 N-B3	N-B3

The immediate development of all four Knights gives the opening its name.

4 B-N5	B-N5
5 Castles	Castles

See Diagram 226.

If White is heading for a draw, he can play 6 BxN, QPxB;

7 NxP, BxN; 8 QPxB, NxP which results in a symmetrical (and lifeless) position.

6   P-Q3   P-Q3

Here too White can choose a symmetrical line (7 N-K2, N-K2; 8 N-N3, N-N3) which involves no lively complications.

7   B-N5   ....

This pin threatens to become annoying, since White is on the point of playing N-Q5. Such a move would threaten the win of

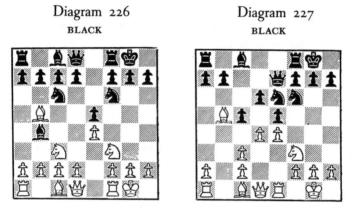

Diagram 226
BLACK

Diagram 227
BLACK

WHITE *to move*   WHITE *to move*

Should White rely on sym-   Black has set a clever trap
metry?

a piece and would force the break-up of Black's Pawns in front of his castled position.

7   ....   BxN

The simplest way to parry White's threats.

8   PxB   ....

Now White has two Bishops against Black's Bishop and Knight. This is considered a minimal advantage, but only if the Bishops have considerable scope, which does not seem to be the case here.

8 .... Q-K2

The beginning of an interesting maneuver. Black sees that White is bound to play P-Q4 to try to open up the position in order to give his Bishops more scope. Black, therefore, takes steps to keep the position closed.

9 R-K1 N-Q1

This Knight is headed for the King 3 square.

10 P-Q4 N-K3
11 B-QB1 ....

Now it seems that Black has nothing better than 11 ... PxP. Then, after 12 PxP, White has a broad Pawn center plus freedom of action for his Bishops; further gain of terrain is promised by the aggressive advance of White's King Pawn.

But Black is well aware of the danger.

11 .... P-B4!

A clever move. White dare not win a Pawn with 12 PxP, PxP; 13 NxP? because 13 ... N-B2 wins a piece. See Diagram 227.

By playing 11 ... P-B4! Black manages to hold on to his King Pawn, which means that the position will remain closed and that White's Bishops will be unable to acquire the scope they need to make their power felt.

RUY LOPEZ

This is the strongest, most complicated, and most interesting opening beginning with 1 P-K4, P-K4. The many problems that it sets both players call for a real mastery of strategical and tactical play.

WHITE	BLACK
1 P-K4	P-K4
2 N-KB3	N-QB3
3 B-N5	. . . .

This is the characteristic move of the Ruy Lopez. Black has defended his King Pawn with 2 . . . N-QB3. Now White plays 3 B-N5, threatening 4 BxN and removing the protector of the King Pawn to make 5 NxP possible.

Does this then mean that White is threatening to win a Pawn? At this stage the answer is no.

3   . . . .   P-QR3!

Black does not fear 4 BxN, QPxB; 5 NxP; for he can recover the Pawn with 5 . . . Q-Q5 or 5 . . . Q-N4.

White's hope is that sooner or later he will truly be threatening to win the Pawn and will thereby induce Black to constrict his game with the protective . . . P-Q3.

Black, on the other hand, is prepared to drive the annoying Bishop away with . . . P-QN4.

4 B-R4   N-B3

Black develops the Knight, gaining time and countering with an attack against White's King Pawn.

White can defend his King Pawn with such moves as 5 P-Q3 or 5 N-B3 or 5 Q-K2. Instead, he prefers a more complicated line of play.

5 Castles   . . . .

See Diagram 228.

Black can now play 5 . . . NxP to which White replies 6 P-Q4.

In that case it is too dangerous to continue 6 ... PxP because of the pinning reply 7 R-K1.

So, after 5 ... NxP; 6 P-Q4; the standard continuation is 6 ... P-QN4; 7 B-N3, P-Q4; 8 PxP, B-K3; 9 P-B3—with about equal chances.

We shall instead follow the more solid and conservative line of play.

5	....	B-K2

Black develops a piece and prepares to castle.

6	R-K1	....

White in turn gives his King Pawn solid protection. Now he really threatens 7 BxN followed by 8 NxP winning a Pawn. Black meets the threat with:

6	....	P-QN4
7	B-N3	P-Q3

This move is inevitable, although it imparts a certain passive and constricted quality to Black's position.

8	P-B3	....

White intends to build a broad Pawn center with P-Q4.

8	....	Castles
9	P-KR3	....

After the immediate 9 P-Q4, the pin 9 ... B-N5 would be annoying. White, therefore, rules out the pin.

9	....	N-QR4!

Black has no intention of being reduced to complete passivity, and he begins an interesting maneuver to give his pieces more space on the Queen-side.

10	B-B2	P-B4
11	P-Q4	Q-B2!

Black avoids ... KPxP, which would open up the center and give White great freedom of action. He plays 11 ... Q-B2! in order to maintain his King Pawn at the King 4 square, keeping the center intact and holding a fairly closed position. (For this reason this is known as the Strong-Point Variation.)

12	QN-Q2	N-B3
13	P-Q5	....

White barricades the center in order to deprive Black of counterplay in the center.

13	....	N-Q1

See Diagram 229.

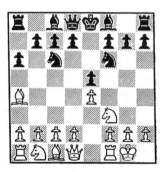

Diagram 228
BLACK *to move*

WHITE

Should Black capture the King Pawn?

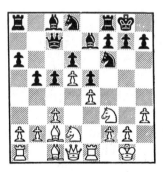

Diagram 229
BLACK

WHITE *to move*

A difficult maneuvering position

Black's position is now cramped, but he is well ensconced in a hedgehog position, and it is difficult to get at him. A likely continuation is 14 P-QR4, R-N1; 15 P-B4!, P-N5; 16 N-B1, N-K1; 17 P-N4, P-N3; 18 B-R6, N-KN2. This results in a difficult situation with complicated maneuvering possibilities.

In the next and final chapter we shall run through some games to provide you with a feeling for practical play. In each case we will find that one of the players makes a serious mistake and that this mistake is directly responsible for his defeat. This clear-cut relationship will underline the fact that chess is a game in which logic predominates.

TENTH REVIEW TEST
(answers on pages 177–178)

1. An _____ is a standardized pattern of beginning moves.
2. The _____ _____ starts with the moves 1 P-K4, P-K4; 2 P-Q4.
3. It is almost always a mistake to develop the _____ early in the game.
4. [Diagram 212] Black threatens to play ... _____.
5. [Diagram 212] If White plays Q-B3, Black wins the Queen with ... _____.
6. [Diagram 213] Assuming that play continues 8 B-B4, BxN; 9 BxB; Black (should/should not) play 9 ... RxP. Reason?
7. A _____ is an opening in which a player sacrifices material in the hope of securing a compensating advantage.
8. The _____ _____ begins with the moves 1 P-K4, P-K4; 2 P-Q4, PxP; 3 P-QB3.
9. The _____ _____ involves the speculative offer of White's King Bishop Pawn in order to remove Black's King Pawn from the center.
10. The _____ _____ begins with the moves 1 P-K4, P-K4; 2 P-KB4.
11. After 1 P-K4, P-K4; 2 P-KB4, PxP; 3 P-Q4; Black has a strong continuation in 3 ... _____.

12. When a Bishop is played to King Knight 2 or Queen Knight 2, we say it has been _____.

13. [Diagram 217] If White answers 8 . . . N-R4 with 9 NxNP, the sequel would be 9 . . . N-N6; 10 R-R2, Q-K2ch. Now if White plays (a) 10 B-K2, Black replies 10 . . . _____ and wins; (b) 10 K-Q2, Black replies 10 . . . _____ and wins, as 11 _____ can be answered by 11 . . . _____; (c) 10 K-B2, Q-K5; 11 P-B3, P-KR4; 12 N-K5; Black replies 12 . . . _____ and wins, as 13 _____ can be answered by 13 . . . _____ and wins; (d) 10 K-B2, Q-K5; 11 P-B3, P-KR4; 12 N-Q2; Black replies 12 . . . _____ winning at least a piece.

14. The _____ _____ _____ starts with the moves 1 P-K4, P-K4; 2 P-KB4, B-B4.

15. [Diagram 218] After 3 PxP?? Black wins with 3 . . . _____.

16. [Diagram 219] In the event of 9 PxP, PxP; 10 NxP?; Black wins with 10 . . . _____.

17. _____ _____ starts with the moves 1 P-K4, P-K4; 2 N-KB3, P-Q3.

18. [Diagram 220] After 4 . . . B-K2?; 5 PxP, PxP?; White wins with 6 _____.

19. [Diagram 220] After 4 . . . P-QB3; 5 PxP, NxP; 6 NxN, PxN; White wins at least a Pawn with 7 _____. Reason?

20. The _____ _____ begins with 1 P-K4, P-K4; 2 N-KB3, N-QB3; 3 P-Q4.

21. [Diagram 222] Black gains time by attacking White's King Pawn with 4 . . . _____.

22. [Diagram 222] After 4 . . . N-B3; 5 N-QB3, B-N5; Black threatens to win a Pawn because White's Queen Knight is _____ by the Black Bishop at Knight 5.

23. The _____ _____ begins with the moves 1 P-K4, P-K4; 2 N-KB3, N-QB3; 3 B-B4, B-B4.

24. [Diagram 224] After 6 B-K3, BxB; 7 PxB; White has an open _____ _____ file.

25. [Diagram 224] After 6 B-K3, B-N3, White plays 7 P-KR3 in order to prevent the annoying _____ by ... B-N5.

26. The _____ _____ _____ begins with the moves 1 P-K4, P-K4; 2 N-KB3, N-QB3; 3 N-B3, N-B3.

27. [Diagram 226] After 6 BxN, QPxB; 7 NxP; Black recovers his Pawn by 7 ... _____; 8 _____, _____.

28. [Diagram 227] After 12 PxP, PxP; 13 NxP?; Black wins a piece with 13 ... _____. Reason?

29. The _____ _____ begins with the moves 1 P-K4, P-K4; 2 N-KB3, N-QB3; 3 B-N5.

30. If Black then replies 3 ... P-QR3 and the game continues 4 BxN; QPxB; 5 NxP; Black recovers his Pawn with 5 ... _____ or 5 ... _____.

31. [Diagram 228] After 5 ... B-K2; 6 R-K1, P-QN4; 7 B-N3, P-Q3; 8 P-Q4, NxQP; 9 NxN, PxN; 10 QxP?; Black wins a piece by 10 ... _____ followed by 11 ... _____.

32. [Diagram 228] After 5 ... B-K2; 6 R-K1; White threatens to win a Pawn by 7 _____ followed by 8 _____.

33. [Diagram 228] After 5 ... B-K2; 6 R-K1, P-QN4; 7 B-N3, P-Q3; 8 P-B3, Castles; 9 P-KR3, N-QR4!; 10 B-B2, P-B4; 11 P-Q4, Q-B2!; 12 QN-Q2, N-B3; 13 N-B1, BPxP; 14 PxP, PxP; 15 NxP?; Black wins a piece by 15 ... _____; 16 _____, _____.

Tenth Review Test: Answers

1. opening
2. Center Game
3. Queen
4. NxQ
5. B-N5
6. should not; White wins a piece with 10 BxN
7. gambit
8. Danish Gambit
9. King's Gambit
10. King's Gambit
11. Q-R5ch

12. fianchettoed
13. (a) 10 ... BxN
    (b) 10 ... Q-N5ch; 11
        K-Q3, B-B4 mate
    (c) 12 ... BxN; 13 PxB,
        QxB
    (d) 12 ... BxN
14. King's Gambit Declined
15. Q-R5ch
16. Q-Q5
17. Philidor's Defense
18. Q-Q5
19. BxPch! as 7 ... KxB??
    allows 8 QxQ
20. Scotch Game

21. N-B3
22. pinned
23. Giuoco Piano
24. King Bishop
25. pin
26. Four Knights' Game
27. BxN; QPxB, NxP
28. N-B2; Black simultane-
    ously attacks White's
    Knight and King Bishop
29. Ruy Lopez
30. Q-Q5; Q-N4
31. P-B4; P-B5
32. BxN; NxP
33. NxN; QxN, QxB

CHAPTER 8

INSTRUCTIVE GAMES

THE PURPOSE of this chapter is to study the complete game as an organic process. Here we see the opening moves and appraise their likely consequences. We see the early jockeying for advantage, and we are able to judge whether these attempts will succeed or fail. We see the coming of the crisis, when respective resources will either triumph or shrivel. Each game is a kind of sermon which preaches the virtues of effective development and denounces the defects of bad development.

CENTER GAME
(Leipzig, 1903)

WHITE	BLACK
Amateur	*Leonhardt*
1 P-K4	P-K4
2 P-Q4	. . . .

We know (Diagram 212) that this results in a loss of time because it involves early development of White's Queen.

2	PxP
3 QxP	N-QB3

Black gains time by attacking the White Queen.

4   Q-K3   N-B3

Black has achieved a substantial lead in development.

5   B-B4   . . . .

White would do better to develop his Queen-side pieces and castle on that wing. See the play from Diagram 212.

5   . . . .   N-K4

Black has just moved his Queen Knight a second time. Generally we would dismiss this as faulty opening play. However,

Diagram 230
BLACK

WHITE *to move*
After 5 . . . N-K4

since White has lost time previously, Black can allow himself this luxury. In addition, Black is attacking White's Bishop, which further minimizes the loss of time involved in the Knight move.

6   B-N3   . . . .

It would have been safer to retreat 6 B-K2, but this would have underlined the pointlessness of White's previous move.

6   ....   B-N5ch

This crafty move is best answered by development, say 7 N-QB3 or 7 B-Q2, after which White would be on the way to closing up the gap in development.

7   P-QB3   ....

But this mechanical reply does not help White's development and, in fact, invites trouble.

7   ....   B-B4!

This tricky move invites 8 QxB? which would cost White his Queen. The same is true of 8 Q-B4?

White's safest retreat would have been 8 Q-K2. But even this comparatively safe move might be objected to, because it would mean that White would have to move his Queen three times to reach a square which originally could have been reached in one move. In any event, Black would still have maintained a commanding lead in development.

8   Q-N3??   ....

In making this attractive move, White is under the mistaken impression that he is gaining time by attacking the advanced Black Knight.

9   ....   BxPch!!
    Resigns

A surprise finish. The point is that the Bishop check attacks White's King and Queen; hence, the Bishop must be captured. However, either way of capturing exposes White to a Knight

Diagram 231

BLACK *to move*

WHITE

After 8 Q-N3??

forking check which forces the win of White's Queen. Consequently, White surrenders with what at first seems surprising suddenness.

A drastic lesson on the consequences of dawdling development.

GIUOCO PIANO
(Berlin, 1907)

WHITE	BLACK
Scheve	*Teichmann*
1 P-K4	P-K4
2 N-KB3	N-QB3
3 B-B4	B-B4
4 P-B3	. . . .

This is a departure from the Giuoco Piano line that we studied earlier. See Diagram 224.

Here White proposes to set up a broad Pawn center with P-Q4.

4 . . . .   Q-K2

In the event of P-Q4, Black has no intention of replying . . . PxP, for then White would obtain a very powerful game with

PxP. Instead, Black intends to answer P-Q4 with ... B-N3, maintaining his hold on the center.

Diagram 232

BLACK

WHITE *to move*

After 4 ... Q-K2

5   Castles   P-Q3

And now Black is quite content with the possibility 6 P-Q4, B-N3; 7 PxP, PxP by which he maintains a firm hold on the center.

6   P-Q4   B-N3
7   P-QR4   ....

Very tricky. White threatens 8 P-R5, BxRP?; 9 P-Q5 winning a piece. There is also another threat: 8 P-R5, NxRP; 9 RxN, BxR; 10 Q-R4ch by which White wins the loose Bishop and remains ahead in material with two minor pieces for a Rook and Pawn.

7   ....   P-QR3

Black parries the threat.

8   P-R5   B-R2

After 8 ... NxRP; 9 RxN, BxR; 10 Q-R4ch, P-QN4; 11
QxB, PxB; 12 Q-R4ch followed by QxBP; White has two Pawns
for the Exchange, and the outcome is unclear.

9   P-R3   . . . .

This move has good and bad features. White prevents the
annoying pin ... B-N5, but he creates a weakness in his castled
position which can prove very costly under certain conditions.

9   . . . .   N-B3

White should now play 10 R-K1—or even 10 P-Q5 if he is
unwilling to maintain the broad Pawn center.

Diagram 233
BLACK

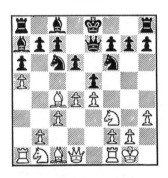

WHITE *to move*
After 9 ... N-B3

10   PxP?   . . . .

Feeble and spineless. Black's pieces suddenly come to life,
particularly his Bishop tucked away at Queen Rook 2. This
Bishop acquires a magnificently elongated diagonal reaching right
down to White King's territory.

10   ....   QNxP

Now this Knight is in good play too. Perhaps White's best reply was 11 B-K2, although the protection of his King Pawn would soon begin to present problems. The initiative has definitely passed to Black.

11   NxN   ....

After this feeble move White is really in trouble.

11   ....   QxN!

Now Black's Queen is powerfully in play. It is true that 12 Q-B3 would prevent Black's next move, but then Black could simply play 12 ... QxKP; 13 QxQ, NxQ; as the pinning move 14 R-K1 would lose for White.

12   N-Q2   ....

Diagram 234
BLACK *to move*

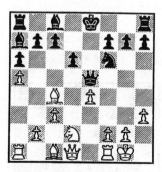

WHITE
After 12 N-Q2

White protects his King Pawn, but he fails to see Black's other threat.

12   ....   BxRP!

Now the weakening of White's castled position comes to light.

White's situation has become very trying. If he plays 13 N-B3, Black wins with 13 ... Q-N6 (threatens ... QxNP mate while White's King Bishop Pawn is pinned, so that 14 PxQ is out of the question); 14 N-K1, N-N5.

Another possibility is 13 Q-B3, B-N5; 14 Q-Q3, Castles/K; and Black is a Pawn ahead with a fine game.

13   PxB   ....

After this White is definitely lost, since his castled position is open to the enemy.

13   ....   Q-N6ch

The point: White's pinned King Bishop Pawn cannot capture the Queen.

14   K-R1   QxRPch
15   K-N1   N-N5

Diagram 235
BLACK

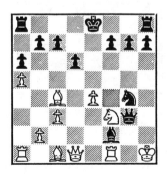

WHITE *to move*
After 17 ... BxP

Threatening mate.

	16 N-B3	Q-N6ch

See the note to Black's thirteenth move.

	17 K-R1	BxP

White resigns, as he has no good defense against the threat of 18 ... Q-R6ch and mate next move. After 18 B-B4, QxB, White would be defenseless against the coming 19 ... Q-N6.

The combination of 10 PxP? and 13 PxB proved fatal for White. The first of these moves opened up the terrible diagonal for Black's King Bishop; the second left White's castled position exposed to crushing attack.

RUY LOPEZ
(Match, 1893)

WHITE	BLACK
Tarrasch	*Tchigorin*
1 P-K4	P-K4
2 N-KB3	N-QB3
3 B-N5	P-QR3
4 B-R4	N-B3
5 N-B3	....

In modern play the alternative 5 Castles is customary.

	5	B-N5

This is out of place here; Black should play 5 ... B-K2.

	6 N-Q5!	....

A difficult move to answer effectively. For example, if 6 ... NxN; 7 PxN, N-K2; 8 NxP, NxP; 9 B-N3; and Black is in trouble.

6	....	B-R4?

After this the Bishop is out of play for the rest of the game. The right move was 6 ... B-K2.

7	Castles	P-QN4
8	B-N3	P-Q3
9	P-Q3	B-KN5

Diagram 236

BLACK

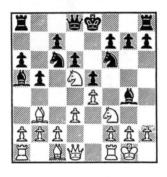

WHITE *to move*
After 9 ... B-KN5

Having pinned White's King Knight, Black is now ready to play ... N-Q5 in order to break up the Pawns in front of White's castled position. To prevent this, White plays:

10	P-B3	....

Black would like to castle, but then comes 11 B-N5 forcing the break-up of Black's King-side Pawns.

Black's safest course was doubtless 10 ... P-R3 (preventing B-N5) followed by castling.

10	....	N-K2??

Black sees that after 10 ... NxN; 11 BxN, Q-Q2; 12 BxN, QxB; 13 NxP!, BxQ; 14 NxQ; White would win material because both Black Bishops would be under attack. (Note how the unfortunate position of Black's Bishop on Queen Rook 4 continues to cause trouble!)

However, the plausible move actually played by Black is also a dangerous one.

Diagram 237

BLACK

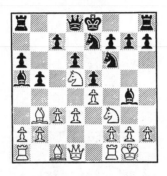

WHITE *to move*
After 10 ... N-K2??

11   NxKP!!   ....

An astonishing offer of the Queen. The point is that after 11 ... BxQ; 12 NxNch, PxN??; there follows 13 BxPch, K-B1; 14 B-R6 mate.

11   ....   PxN

To be sure, Black can put up a more stubborn defense with 11 ... BxQ; 12 NxNch, K-B1; 13 N/K5-Q7ch, QxN; 14 NxQch, K-K1; 15 RxB, KxN. However, with a Pawn down Black would be certain to lose the ensuing endgame.

12   NxNch   ....

By capturing this Knight with check, White gains the time to capture the Black Bishop.

12   ....   PxN
13   QxB   ....

Thus, White remains a Pawn ahead, as 13 ... QxP?? would be ruinous for Black.

Note that Black cannot castle. It will soon become apparent that his King is exposed to a dangerous attack.

13   ....   N-N3
14   B-Q5   QR-N1
15   P-KB4!   ....

Diagram 238
BLACK *to move*

WHITE
After 15 P-KB4!

If Black castles now, he loses a piece. With his King forced to remain in the center, he will soon be exposed to a withering attack along the King Bishop file.

15   ....   P-B3

Black gives away a second Pawn, hoping for complications.

<table>
<tr><td>16</td><td>BxQBPch</td><td>K-K2</td></tr>
</table>

And now of course Black can never castle. At the moment he threatens ... Q-N3ch with a double attack which would win White's advanced Bishop. Naturally White avoids this possibility.

<table>
<tr><td>17</td><td>B-Q5</td><td>P-N5</td></tr>
<tr><td>18</td><td>PxKP</td><td>Q-N3ch</td></tr>
<tr><td>19</td><td>K-R1</td><td>NxP</td></tr>
<tr><td>20</td><td>Q-R5</td><td>....</td></tr>
</table>

White is getting to work in earnest. He threatens 21 RxP!! (note the good work along the open King Bishop file), so that if 21 ... KxR; then 22 Q-N5 mate—or 21 ... QxR; then 22 B-N5, winning Black's Queen.

<table>
<tr><td>20</td><td>....</td><td>N-N3</td></tr>
</table>

Diagram 239
BLACK *to move*

WHITE
After 20 ... N-N3

<table>
<tr><td>21</td><td>RxP!!</td><td>....</td></tr>
</table>

This still works, thanks to the exposed state of Black's King and the disorganized state of his other forces.

21   ....   KxR

What now follows is a classic example of concentrated attack against a helpless King.

22 B-N5ch   K-N2

The alternative 22 . . . K-K4 lets White mate in two moves.

23 Q-R6ch   K-N1
24 R-KB1   ....

Triumph of the open King Bishop file. White threatens mate on the move.

24   ....   R-KB1
25 B-KB6   ....

Once more White threatens mate on the move.

25   ....   QxB

Diagram 240
BLACK *to move*

WHITE
After 26 RxQ

The only defense, for the moment.

26 RxQ   Resigns

Black realizes that he is defenseless against the threat of 27 RxNch!, RPxN; 28 QxP mate.

Note that Black's misplaced Bishop remained useless to the very end of the game.

QUEEN FIANCHETTO DEFENSE
(Philadelphia, 1859)
[White plays blindfold]

WHITE	BLACK
Morphy	*Lewis*
1 P-K4	P-QN3

This is our first game in which Black refuses to answer 1 P-K4 with 1 ... P-K4. The move he has selected is too passive, because it gives White a completely free hand in the center.

2 P-Q4   ....

White immediately forms a broad Pawn center.

2	B-N2
3 B-Q3	P-K3
4 N-KR3!	....

An unusual and highly interesting move. Morphy was of course well aware that a Knight is generally poorly placed at the side of the board. His object here was to make room for the advance of his King Bishop Pawn. (This would be ruled out by the more orthodox 4 N-KB3.)

As for the Knight at the side of the board, White foresees a brilliant future for him.

4   ....   P-Q4

Rather late in the day Black decides to make a stand in the
center. However, this turns out badly.

5   P-K5!   ....

Diagram 241
BLACK *to move*

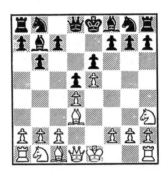

WHITE
After 5 P-K5!

White has a distinct advantage. Black's Queen Bishop has no
scope and his King-side pieces have miserable prospects. White's
Pawn wedge at King 5 heralds a King-side attack—if only because this Pawn prevents Black from developing his King Knight
to King Bishop 3, the most effective defensive post for this Knight.

5   ....   N-K2

Note by the way that while Black's fianchettoed Bishop at
Queen Knight 2 is shut out of the game, White's Bishop at Queen
3 has a magnificent diagonal.

6   Castles   N-N3
7   P-KB4!   ....

Very well played. White intends to push the Pawn ahead, opening the King Bishop file for attacking purposes. In doing so, he is carrying out the underlying idea behind 4 N-KR3!

7	....	B-K2
8	P-B5!	PxP
9	BxP	B-B1

Not a bad idea. Since this Bishop is destined to be useless, Black exchanges him for White's valuable Bishop. Unfortunately, this sensible maneuver does not prove too helpful, because White's lead in development and mobility still remains substantial.

10	BxB	QxB
11	N-B3	....

Morphy's specialty: developing and gaining time.

11	....	P-QB3
12	B-N5!	Castles
13	BxB	NxB

Diagram 242

BLACK

WHITE *to move*

After 13 ... NxB

14   Q-R5!   . . . .

White has formidable attacking prospects based on the aggressive position of his Queen and his control of the open King Bishop file.

White now threatens to win at least a Pawn by 15 N-KN5 (threatening mate), P-KR3; 16 NxBP, etc.

Black loses quickly after 14 . . . P-N3; 15 Q-R6, N-B4; 16 RxN!, QxR; 17 N-KN5, R-K1; 18 R-KB1, etc.

Also if 14 . . . Q-K3; 15 R-B3!, N-Q2; 16 QR-KB1; the pressure on the King Bishop file must be decisive. If Black tries to neutralize it with 16 . . . P-B3, then 17 N-B4! wins—for example, 17 . . . Q-B4; 18 QxQ, NxQ; 19 N-K6, etc.; or 17 . . . Q-B2; 18 QxQch, etc.

14   . . . .   P-KR3

Black prevents N-KN5, but at the cost of weakening his castled position. The ensuing play is a good example of how one can take advantage of such a weakening.

15   R-B3!   . . . .

White prepares to double Rooks on the King Bishop file, and he also contemplates R-N3 threatening QxRP and, thus, exploiting the weakness created by 14 . . . P-KR3.

15   . . . .   N-N3

This is intended to neutralize some of White's pressure on the King Bishop and King Knight files.

16   QR-KB1!   Q-K3

Both players have made their dispositions for the coming phase. White has the upper hand because both of his Rooks are in the fray while Black has only one Rook doing defensive work.

Diagram 243

BLACK

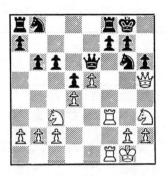

WHITE *to move*

After 16 ... Q-K3

| 17 | N-K2! | .... |

White proceeds to remove Black's defensive Knight in order to increase his overwhelming superiority on the King-side.

17	....	N-Q2
18	N/K2-B4!	NxN
19	NxN	Q-K2
20	R-KN3	....

White threatens 21 QxRP. Now that Black's protective Knight has disappeared, his King-side must collapse under the pressure.

| 20 | .... | K-R2 |

This parries the threat, but there will be new ones.

| 21 | R/B1-B3! | .... |

This renews the pressure with a vengeance.

White now threatens 22 RxPch!, KxR; 23' R-KN3ch. Thus if 23 ... K-R2; 24 R-KR3 wins, as 24 ... Q-N4 is useless.

Again, if 23 ... Q-N4; then 24 RxQch, PxR; 25 QxNPch. Now further Queen checks will win Black's Knight, leaving White with a comfortable advantage in material.

Diagram 244

BLACK

WHITE *to move*

After 21 R/B1-B3!

Black cannot defend himself with 21 ... P-N3, for then White wins with 22 NxNP, PxN; 23 RxP, etc.

21	....	R-KN1
22	N-R3!	....

White's principal threat is now 23 N-N5ch, K-R1; 24 NxPch, K-R2; 25 Q-N6 mate.

22	....	P-N3
23	N-N5ch!	....

This leaves Black no choice, for after 23 ... K-N2; 24 RxPch, QxR; 25 NxQ; Black is unable to play 25 ... PxQ.

23.	....	QxN
24	RxPch	....

And now if 24 ... R-N2; 25 RxRch, KxR; 26 RxQ; Black cannot play 26 ... PxQ. If he plays 26 ... PxR; White replies 27 QxP/N5 with an easy win.

24	....	K-R1

Now White can win easily with 25 RxQ, PxQ; 26 RxRch followed by 27 RxN. But he does much better:

25	QxQ!	Resigns

For if 25 ... PxQ; 26 R-KR3 mate. The faultless and efficient manner in which White carried out the attack is beyond all praise.

Diagram 245
BLACK *to move*

WHITE
After 25 QxQ!

SICILIAN DEFENSE
(National Intercollegiate
Championship, 1929)

WHITE	BLACK
Reinfeld	*Grossman*
1 P-K4	P-QB4

Here too Black avoids playing 1 ... P-K4. But at least 1 ...
P-QB4 makes more sense than 1 ... P-QN3, for the advance of
Black's Queen Bishop Pawn restrains White from forming a
broad Pawn center with P-Q4.

2	N-KB3	N-QB3
3	P-Q4	. . . .

Since the threatened P-Q5 would stifle Black's game, he
naturally exchanges Pawns.

3	. . . .	PxP
4	NxP	. . . .

As a result of the exchange of Pawns, White has a half-open
Queen file while Black has a half-open Queen Bishop file. Each
player hopes to put the half-open file to good use.

4	. . . .	N-B3
5	N-QB3	P-Q3
6	B-K2	P-QR3

Black wants to play ...Q-B2 without having his Queen dis-
turbed by N-N5.

7	Castles	Q-B2

It would have been safer to play ... P-K3 in order to prevent
White's next move. Instead, Black deliberately courts this move
in order to win a Pawn.

8	N-Q5!	KNxN
9	PxN	NxN
10	QxN	QxP?

Black has lost valuable time and soon finds himself consider-
ably behind in development.

Diagram 246

BLACK

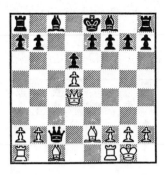

WHITE *to move*

After 10 ... QxP

11	B-QB4	Q-N3

Black loses more time with the Queen, but he has little choice.
His prime difficulty is that he cannot develop his King Bishop;
this makes it impossible for him to castle and leaves his King
vulnerable to attack.

12	B-B4	Q-B3
13	Q-K3	....

It is clearly in White's interest to avoid the exchange of
Queens. Black might now try 13 ... P-R3; 14 KR-K1, P-KN4
(if 14 ... QxP; 15 BxQP); 15 B-KN3, B-N2; but after 16 Q-
N6, Castles; 17 Q-B7; White has all the play.

13	....	P-K4
14	PxP e.p.!	....

Very important. If White is to make his advantage in mobility
tell, he must open new lines.

14	....	BxP

15	KR-K1	K-Q2
16	B-KN5!	Q-B4
17	Q-N6!	. . . .

Diagram 247
BLACK *to move*

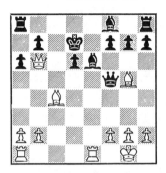

WHITE
After 17 Q-N6!

White's offer of both Bishops comes as a stunning surprise, but it is actually grounded on strict logic.

If Black plays 17 . . . BxB, White replies 18 QxNP mate.

If Black plays 17 . . . QxB, White replies 18 QxNPch and then captures Black's Rook with check.

| 17 | . . . . | R-B1 |

Black does no better with 17 . . . QR-N1 in view of 18 BxBch, PxB; 19 QR-B1 with the irresistible threat of 20 Q-B7ch.

The fact is that the dangerous position of Black's King in the center exposes him to one vicious threat after another.

| 18 | BxBch | PxB |
| 19 | QR-B1 | . . . . |

White can afford to ignore the attack on his Bishop as he threatens 20 QxNPch followed by 21 RxR mate.

| 19 | .... | Q-N4 |

This is the only defense, but White has a powerful reply.

| 20 | Q-K3! | .... |

Diagram 248
BLACK *to move*

WHITE
After 20 Q-K3!

Threatening 21 QxP mate.

Note that 20 ... P-K4 cannot be played, as it would lead to 21 Q-KR3ch, K-K1; 22 Q-K6ch and mate next move.

Or 20 ... Q-KB4; 21 RxR, KxR; 22 R-QB1ch, K-N1; 23 B-Q8! and Black is lost.

| 20 | .... | R-K1 |

He parries the mate threat but in so doing he surrenders the Queen Bishop file.

| 21 | R-B3! | .... |

White intends to play 22 KR-QB1 with the terrible threat of R-B7 mate.

21   ....   P-Q4

Now Black can answer 22 KR-QB1 with 22 ... B-Q3. So White selects a different way, involving magnificent *centralizing* of his Queen.

22 Q-K5!   ....

With a double mate threat.

22   ....   Q-N3

Or 22 ... B-Q3; 23 QxNPch, B-K2; 24 BxB, KR-N1; 25 Q-B7 and wins, as 25 ... RxB is answered by 26 QxR/N8.

23 KR-QB1   Resigns

Diagram 249
BLACK *to move*

WHITE
After 23 KR-QB1

Black is helpless against the threat of 24 R-B7ch followed by mate next move. If Black tries 23 ... B-Q3, then 24 QxNPch, B-K2; 25 BxB is crushing.

A very instructive game because of White's skill in using the open lines against Black's hapless King. Note that it was Black's

ill-judged 10 ... QxP? that opened the Queen Bishop file for
White.

ELEVENTH REVIEW TEST
(answers on pages 207–208)

1. The _____ _____ begins with the moves
   1 P-K4, P-K4; 2 P-Q4.
2. In this opening White makes the mistake of developing his
   _____ prematurely.
3. [Diagram 230] Black threatens 6 ... _____ .
4. [Diagram 230] After 6 B-N3, B-N5ch; 7 P-QB3, B-B4!; 8
   QxB; Black wins White's Queen with 8 ... _____ .
5. [Diagram 230] After 6 B-N3, B-N5ch; 7 P-QB3, B-B4!; 8
   Q-B4; Black wins White's Queen with 8 ... _____ .
6. [Diagram 231] After 9 ... BxPch!!; 10 QxB; Black wins
   White's Queen with 10 ... _____ .
7. [Diagram 231] After 9 ... BxPch!!; 10 KxB; Black wins
   White's Queen with 10 ... _____ .
8. The _____ _____ begins with the moves
   1 P-K4, P- K4; 2 N-KB3, N-QB3; 3 B-B4, B-B4.
9. [Diagram 233] After 10 PxP?, QNxP; 11 NxN, QxN!; 12
   Q-B3, QxKP; 13 QxQ, NxQ; 14 R-K1; Black wins with
   14 ... _____ .
10. [Diagram 234] If 12 ... NxP; 13 NxN, QxN; White wins
    with 14 _____ .
11. [Diagram 234] After 12 ... BxRP!; 13 PxB, Q-N6ch; 14
    K-R1, QxRPch; 15 K-N1, N-N5; Black threatens 16 ...
    _____ .
12. [Diagram 238] After 15 ... Castles, White wins a piece
    with 16 _____ .
13. The _____ _____ begins with the moves
    1 P-K4, P-K4; 2 N-KB3, N-QB3; 3 B-N5.
14. [Diagram 238] After 15 ... P-B3; 16 BxQBPch, K-K2; 17
    B-Q5, P-N5; 18 PxKP, Q-N3ch; 19 K-R1, NxP; 20 Q-R5;
    White threatens 21 RxP!!, QxR; 22 B-N5 pinning Black's
    _____ .

15. [Diagram 239] After 21 RxP!!, KxR; 22 B-N5ch, K-K4;
    White mates with 23 ——————, ——————; 24
    ——————.

16. [Diagram 239] After 21 RxP!!, KxR; 22 B-N5ch, K-N2; 23
    Q-R6ch, K-N1; 24 R-KB1; White threatens 25 ——————.

17. [Diagram 239] After 21 RxP!!, KxR; 22 B-N5ch, K-N2; 23
    Q-R6ch, K-N1; 24 R-KB1, R-KB1; 25 B-KB6; White
    threatens 26 ——————. .

18. [Diagram 240] White threatens 27 RxNch!, RPxN; 28 QxP
    mate because Black's Bishop Pawn is —————— by
    White's Bishop.

19. The —————— —————— —————— be-
    gins with the moves 1 P-K4, P-QN3.

20. The drawback to 1 ... P-QN3 is that it gives White a com-
    pletely free hand in the ——————.

21. [Diagram 241] With 4 ... P-Q4, Black has blocked the
    diagonal of his —————— ——————.

22. [Diagram 241] White's Pawn at King 5 prevents Black from
    playing his Knight to —————— —————— ——————.

23. [Diagram 241] After 5 ... N-K2; 6 Castles, N-N3; 7 P-
    KB4!; White plans to open the —————— —————— file.

24. [Diagram 242] After 14 Q-R5! White intends 15 N-KN5
    threatening 16 ——————.

25. [Diagram 242] After 14 Q-R5!, Q-K3; 15 R-B3!, N-Q2; 16
    QR-KB1, P-B3; 17 N-B4!, Q-B4; 18 QxQ, NxQ; 19 N-K6;
    White wins the ——————.

26. [Diagram 242] In the above line, if Black plays 18 ... Q-B2,
    White wins with 19 QxQch followed by 20 ——————
    winning a piece.

27. [Diagram 243] After 17 N-K2!, N-Q2; 18 N/K2-B4!, NxN;
    19 NxN, Q-K2; 20 R-KN3, K-R2; 21 R/B1-B3!; White
    threatens 22 RxPch!; KxR; 23 R-KN3ch, K-R2; 24 R-KR3,
    as 24 ... Q-N4 would be refuted by 25 ——————.

28. [Diagram 243] In the above line, if 23 ... Q-N4; 24 RxQch,
    PxR; 25 QxNPch, K-R1; White wins the Black Knight by
    26 —————— or —————— followed by 27
    ——————.

29. [Diagram 244] After 21 ... P-N3; 22 NxNP, PxN; 23 RxP; Black must defend the mate with 23 ... Q-N2; but then White wins with 24 RxQch, KxR; 25 _____ and 26 _____.

30. [Diagram 244] After 23 ... K-N2; 24 RxPch, QxR; 25 NxQ; Black is unable to play 25 ... PxQ because his King Knight Pawn is _____ by White's _____.

31. The _____ _____ begins with the moves 1 P-K4, P-QB4.

32. After 1 P-K4, P-QB4; 2 N-KB3, N-QB3; 3 P-Q4; White threatens to stifle Black's game with 4 _____.

33. [Diagram 246] After 11 B-QB4, Q-N3; 12 B-B4, Q-B3; 13 Q-K3, P-K4; 14 PxP e.p.!, BxP; White plays 15 KR-K1 to strengthen his _____ on Black's Queen Bishop.

34. [Diagram 247] After 17 ... R-B1; 18 BxBch, PxB; 19 QxNPch; Black beats off the attack with 19 ... _____.

35. [Diagram 248] After 20 ... R-K1; 21 R-B3!, P-Q4; 22 Q-K5!, B-B4; White has a winning reply in 23 _____.

36. [Diagram 249] After 23 ... Q-Q3, there follows 24 _____, _____; 25 _____ or _____.

Eleventh Review Test: Answers

1. Center Game	10. R-K 1
2. Queen	11. Q-R7 mate
3. NxB	12. Castles; P-B5
4. N-Q6ch	13. Ruy Lopez
5. N-Q6ch	14. B-N5
6. N-Q6ch	15. B-K7 dis ch, P-B4; QxBP mate
7. NxPch	
8. Giuoco Piano	16. BxP mate
9. BxPch	17. Q-N7 mate

18. pinned
19. Queen Fianchetto Defense
20. center
21. Queen Bishop
22. King Bishop 3
23. King Bishop
24. QxRP mate
25. Exchange
26. P-K6
27. QxQ

28. Q-R4ch; Q-R5ch; Q-N4ch
29. Q-N4ch; QxN
30. pinned; Rook
31. Sicilian Defense
32. P-Q5
33. pin
34. R-B 2
35. QxNPch
36. R-B7ch, QxR; RxQ mate or QxQ mate

INDEX

MELVIN POWERS SELF-IMPROVEMENT LIBRARY

ASTROLOGY

____ ASTROLOGY: HOW TO CHART YOUR HOROSCOPE *Max Heindel*	5.00
____ ASTROLOGY AND SEXUAL ANALYSIS *Morris C. Goodman*	5.00
____ ASTROLOGY AND YOU *Carroll Righter*	5.00
____ ASTROLOGY MADE EASY *Astarte*	5.00
____ ASTROLOGY, ROMANCE, YOU AND THE STARS *Anthony Norvell*	5.00
____ MY WORLD OF ASTROLOGY *Sydney Omarr*	7.00
____ THOUGHT DIAL *Sydney Omarr*	7.00
____ WHAT THE STARS REVEAL ABOUT THE MEN IN YOUR LIFE *Thelma White*	3.00

BRIDGE

____ BRIDGE BIDDING MADE EASY *Edwin B. Kantar*	10.00
____ BRIDGE CONVENTIONS *Edwin B. Kantar*	10.00
____ COMPETITIVE BIDDING IN MODERN BRIDGE *Edgar Kaplan*	7.00
____ DEFENSIVE BRIDGE PLAY COMPLETE *Edwin B. Kantar*	15.00
____ GAMESMAN BRIDGE—PLAY BETTER WITH KANTAR *Edwin B. Kantar*	7.00
____ HOW TO IMPROVE YOUR BRIDGE *Alfred Sheinwold*	7.00
____ IMPROVING YOUR BIDDING SKILLS *Edwin B. Kantar*	7.00
____ INTRODUCTION TO DECLARER'S PLAY *Edwin B. Kantar*	7.00
____ INTRODUCTION TO DEFENDER'S PLAY *Edwin B. Kantar*	7.00
____ KANTAR FOR THE DEFENSE *Edwin B. Kantar*	7.00
____ KANTAR FOR THE DEFENSE VOLUME 2 *Edwin B. Kantar*	7.00
____ TEST YOUR BRIDGE PLAY *Edwin B. Kantar*	7.00
____ VOLUME 2—TEST YOUR BRIDGE PLAY *Edwin B. Kantar*	7.00
____ WINNING DECLARER PLAY *Dorothy Hayden Truscott*	10.00

BUSINESS, STUDY & REFERENCE

____ BRAINSTORMING *Charles Clark*	7.00
____ CONVERSATION MADE EASY *Elliot Russell*	5.00
____ EXAM SECRET *Dennis B. Jackson*	5.00
____ FIX-IT BOOK *Arthur Symons*	2.00
____ HOW TO DEVELOP A BETTER SPEAKING VOICE *M. Hellier*	4.00
____ HOW TO SAVE 50% ON GAS & CAR EXPENSES *Ken Stansbie*	5.00
____ HOW TO SELF-PUBLISH YOUR BOOK & MAKE IT A BEST SELLER *Melvin Powers*	20.00
____ INCREASE YOUR LEARNING POWER *Geoffrey A. Dudley*	5.00
____ PRACTICAL GUIDE TO BETTER CONCENTRATION *Melvin Powers*	5.00
____ 7 DAYS TO FASTER READING *William S. Schaill*	7.00
____ SONGWRITERS' RHYMING DICTIONARY *Jane Shaw Whitfield*	10.00
____ SPELLING MADE EASY *Lester D. Basch & Dr. Milton Finkelstein*	3.00
____ STUDENT'S GUIDE TO BETTER GRADES *J. A. Rickard*	3.00
____ TEST YOURSELF—FIND YOUR HIDDEN TALENT *Jack Shafer*	3.00
____ YOUR WILL & WHAT TO DO ABOUT IT *Attorney Samuel G. Kling*	5.00

CALLIGRAPHY

____ ADVANCED CALLIGRAPHY *Katherine Jeffares*	7.00
____ CALLIGRAPHY—THE ART OF BEAUTIFUL WRITING *Katherine Jeffares*	7.00
____ CALLIGRAPHY FOR FUN & PROFIT *Anne Leptich & Jacque Evans*	7.00
____ CALLIGRAPHY MADE EASY *Tina Serafini*	7.00

CHESS & CHECKERS

____ BEGINNER'S GUIDE TO WINNING CHESS *Fred Reinfeld*	7.00
____ CHESS IN TEN EASY LESSONS *Larry Evans*	5.00
____ CHESS MADE EASY *Milton L. Hanauer*	5.00
____ CHESS PROBLEMS FOR BEGINNERS *Edited by Fred Reinfeld*	5.00
____ CHESS TACTICS FOR BEGINNERS *Edited by Fred Reinfeld*	5.00

___ HOW TO WIN AT CHECKERS *Fred Reinfeld*	5.00
___ 1001 BRILLIANT WAYS TO CHECKMATE *Fred Reinfeld*	7.00
___ 1001 WINNING CHESS SACRIFICES & COMBINATIONS *Fred Reinfeld*	7.00

COOKERY & HERBS

___ CULPEPER'S HERBAL REMEDIES *Dr. Nicholas Culpeper*	5.00
___ FAST GOURMET COOKBOOK *Poppy Cannon*	2.50
___ HEALING POWER OF HERBS *May Bethel*	5.00
___ HEALING POWER OF NATURAL FOODS *May Bethel*	7.00
___ HERBS FOR HEALTH—HOW TO GROW & USE THEM *Louise Evans Doole*	5.00
___ HOME GARDEN COOKBOOK—DELICIOUS NATURAL FOOD RECIPES *Ken Kraft*	3.00
___ MEATLESS MEAL GUIDE *Tomi Ryan & James H. Ryan, M.D.*	4.00
___ VEGETABLE GARDENING FOR BEGINNERS *Hugh Wiberg*	2.00
___ VEGETABLES FOR TODAY'S GARDENS *R. Milton Carleton*	2.00
___ VEGETARIAN COOKERY *Janet Walker*	7.00
___ VEGETARIAN COOKING MADE EASY & DELECTABLE *Veronica Vezza*	3.00
___ VEGETARIAN DELIGHTS—A HAPPY COOKBOOK FOR HEALTH *K. R. Mehta*	2.00

GAMBLING & POKER

___ HOW TO WIN AT DICE GAMES *Skip Frey*	3.00
___ HOW TO WIN AT POKER *Terence Reese & Anthony T. Watkins*	7.00
___ SCARNE ON DICE *John Scarne*	15.00
___ WINNING AT CRAPS *Dr. Lloyd T. Commins*	5.00
___ WINNING AT GIN *Chester Wander & Cy Rice*	3.00
___ WINNING AT POKER—AN EXPERT'S GUIDE *John Archer*	5.00
___ WINNING AT 21—AN EXPERT'S GUIDE *John Archer*	7.00
___ WINNING POKER SYSTEMS *Norman Zadeh*	3.00

HEALTH

___ BEE POLLEN *Lynda Lyngheim & Jack Scagnetti*	3.00
___ COPING WITH ALZHEIMER'S *Rose Oliver, Ph.D. & Francis Bock, Ph.D.*	10.00
___ DR. LINDNER'S POINT SYSTEM FOOD PROGRAM *Peter G. Lindner, M.D.*	2.00
___ HELP YOURSELF TO BETTER SIGHT *Margaret Darst Corbett*	7.00
___ HOW YOU CAN STOP SMOKING PERMANENTLY *Ernest Caldwell*	5.00
___ MIND OVER PLATTER *Peter G. Lindner, M.D.*	5.00
___ NATURE'S WAY TO NUTRITION & VIBRANT HEALTH *Robert J. Scrutton*	3.00
___ NEW CARBOHYDRATE DIET COUNTER *Patti Lopez-Pereira*	2.00
___ REFLEXOLOGY *Dr. Maybelle Segal*	5.00
___ REFLEXOLOGY FOR GOOD HEALTH *Anna Kaye & Don C. Matchan*	7.00
___ 30 DAYS TO BEAUTIFUL LEGS *Dr. Marc Selner*	3.00
___ YOU CAN LEARN TO RELAX *Dr. Samuel Gutwirth*	3.00

HOBBIES

___ BEACHCOMBING FOR BEGINNERS *Norman Hickin*	2.00
___ BLACKSTONE'S MODERN CARD TRICKS *Harry Blackstone*	7.00
___ BLACKSTONE'S SECRETS OF MAGIC *Harry Blackstone*	5.00
___ COIN COLLECTING FOR BEGINNERS *Burton Hobson & Fred Reinfeld*	7.00
___ ENTERTAINING WITH ESP *Tony 'Doc' Shiels*	2.00
___ 400 FASCINATING MAGIC TRICKS YOU CAN DO *Howard Thurston*	7.00
___ HOW I TURN JUNK INTO FUN AND PROFIT *Sari*	3.00
___ HOW TO WRITE A HIT SONG & SELL IT *Tommy Boyce*	10.00
___ MAGIC FOR ALL AGES *Walter Gibson*	4.00
___ STAMP COLLECTING FOR BEGINNERS *Burton Hobson*	3.00

HORSE PLAYER'S WINNING GUIDES

___ BETTING HORSES TO WIN *Les Conklin*	7.00
___ ELIMINATE THE LOSERS *Bob McKnight*	5.00
___ HOW TO PICK WINNING HORSES *Bob McKnight*	5.00

___ HOW TO WIN AT THE RACES *Sam (The Genius) Lewin*	5.00
___ HOW YOU CAN BEAT THE RACES *Jack Kavanaqh*	5.00
___ MAKING MONEY AT THE RACES *David Barr*	5.00
___ PAYDAY AT THE RACES *Les Conklin*	5.00
___ SMART HANDICAPPING MADE EASY *William Bauman*	5.00
___ SUCCESS AT THE HARNESS RACES *Barry Meadow*	5.00

HUMOR

___ HOW TO FLATTEN YOUR TUSH *Coach Marge Reardon*	2.00
___ JOKE TELLER'S HANDBOOK *Bob Orben*	7.00
___ JOKES FOR ALL OCCASIONS *Al Schock*	5.00
___ 2,000 NEW LAUGHS FOR SPEAKERS *Bob Orben*	7.00
___ 2,400 JOKES TO BRIGHTEN YOUR SPEECHES *Robert Orben*	7.00
___ 2,500 JOKES TO START 'EM LAUGHING *Bob Orben*	7.00

HYPNOTISM

___ ADVANCED TECHNIQUES OF HYPNOSIS *Melvin Powers*	3.00
___ CHILDBIRTH WITH HYPNOSIS *William S. Kroger, M.D.*	5.00
___ HOW TO SOLVE YOUR SEX PROBLEMS WITH SELF-HYPNOSIS *Frank S. Caprio, M.D.*	5.00
___ HOW TO STOP SMOKING THRU SELF-HYPNOSIS *Leslie M. LeCron*	3.00
___ HOW YOU CAN BOWL BETTER USING SELF-HYPNOSIS *Jack Heise*	4.00
___ HOW YOU CAN PLAY BETTER GOLF USING SELF-HYPNOSIS *Jack Heise*	3.00
___ HYPNOSIS AND SELF-HYPNOSIS *Bernard Hollander, M.D.*	5.00
___ HYPNOTISM *(Originally published in 1893) Carl Sextus*	5.00
___ HYPNOTISM MADE EASY *Dr. Ralph Winn*	5.00
___ HYPNOTISM MADE PRACTICAL *Louis Orton*	5.00
___ HYPNOTISM REVEALED *Melvin Powers*	3.00
___ HYPNOTISM TODAY *Leslie LeCron and Jean Bordeaux, Ph.D.*	5.00
___ MODERN HYPNOSIS *Lesley Kuhn & Salvatore Russo, Ph.D.*	5.00
___ NEW CONCEPTS OF HYPNOSIS *Bernard C. Gindes, M.D.*	10.00
___ NEW SELF-HYPNOSIS *Paul Adams*	7.00
___ POST-HYPNOTIC INSTRUCTIONS—SUGGESTIONS FOR THERAPY *Arnold Furst*	5.00
___ PRACTICAL GUIDE TO SELF-HYPNOSIS *Melvin Powers*	5.00
___ PRACTICAL HYPNOTISM *Philip Magonet, M.D.*	3.00
___ SECRETS OF HYPNOTISM *S. J. Van Pelt, M.D.*	5.00
___ SELF-HYPNOSIS—A CONDITIONED-RESPONSE TECHNIQUE *Laurence Sparks*	7.00
___ SELF-HYPNOSIS—ITS THEORY, TECHNIQUE & APPLICATION *Melvin Powers*	3.00
___ THERAPY THROUGH HYPNOSIS *Edited by Raphael H. Rhodes*	5.00

JUDAICA

___ SERVICE OF THE HEART *Evelyn Garfiel, Ph.D.*	10.00
___ STORY OF ISRAEL IN COINS *Jean & Maurice Gould*	2.00
___ STORY OF ISRAEL IN STAMPS *Maxim & Gabriel Shamir*	1.00
___ TONGUE OF THE PROPHETS *Robert St. John*	7.00

JUST FOR WOMEN

___ COSMOPOLITAN'S GUIDE TO MARVELOUS MEN Foreword by *Helen Gurley Brown*	3.00
___ COSMOPOLITAN'S HANG-UP HANDBOOK Foreword by *Helen Gurley Brown*	4.00
___ COSMOPOLITAN'S LOVE BOOK—A GUIDE TO ECSTASY IN BED	7.00
___ COSMOPOLITAN'S NEW ETIQUETTE GUIDE Foreword by *Helen Gurley Brown*	4.00
___ I AM A COMPLEAT WOMAN *Doris Hagopian & Karen O'Connor Sweeney*	3.00
___ JUST FOR WOMEN—A GUIDE TO THE FEMALE BODY *Richard E. Sand, M.D.*	5.00
___ NEW APPROACHES TO SEX IN MARRIAGE *John E. Eichenlaub, M.D.*	3.00
___ SEXUALLY ADEQUATE FEMALE *Frank S. Caprio, M.D.*	3.00
___ SEXUALLY FULFILLED WOMAN *Dr. Rachel Copelan*	5.00

MARRIAGE, SEX & PARENTHOOD

____ ABILITY TO LOVE *Dr. Allan Fromme*	7.00
____ GUIDE TO SUCCESSFUL MARRIAGE *Drs. Albert Ellis & Robert Harper*	7.00
____ HOW TO RAISE AN EMOTIONALLY HEALTHY, HAPPY CHILD *Albert Ellis, Ph.D.*	7.00
____ PARENT SURVIVAL TRAINING *Marvin Silverman, Ed.D. & David Lustig, Ph.D.*	10.00
____ SEX WITHOUT GUILT *Albert Ellis, Ph.D.*	5.00
____ SEXUALLY ADEQUATE MALE *Frank S. Caprio, M.D.*	3.00
____ SEXUALLY FULFILLED MAN *Dr. Rachel Copelan*	5.00
____ STAYING IN LOVE *Dr. Norton F. Kristy*	7.00

MELVIN POWERS' MAIL ORDER LIBRARY

____ HOW TO GET RICH IN MAIL ORDER *Melvin Powers*	20.00
____ HOW TO SELF-PUBLISH YOUR BOOK & MAKE IT A BEST SELLER *Melvin Powers*	20.00
____ HOW TO WRITE A GOOD ADVERTISEMENT *Victor O. Schwab*	20.00
____ MAIL ORDER MADE EASY *J. Frank Brumbaugh*	20.00

METAPHYSICS & OCCULT

____ CONCENTRATION—A GUIDE TO MENTAL MASTERY *Mouni Sadhu*	7.00
____ EXTRA-TERRESTRIAL INTELLIGENCE—THE FIRST ENCOUNTER	6.00
____ FORTUNE TELLING WITH CARDS *P. Foli*	5.00
____ HOW TO INTERPRET DREAMS, OMENS & FORTUNE TELLING SIGNS *Gettings*	5.00
____ HOW TO UNDERSTAND YOUR DREAMS *Geoffrey A. Dudley*	5.00
____ IN DAYS OF GREAT PEACE *Mouni Sadhu*	3.00
____ MAGICIAN—HIS TRAINING AND WORK *W. E. Butler*	5.00
____ MEDITATION *Mouni Sadhu*	10.00
____ MODERN NUMEROLOGY *Morris C. Goodman*	5.00
____ NUMEROLOGY—ITS FACTS AND SECRETS *Ariel Yvon Taylor*	5.00
____ NUMEROLOGY MADE EASY *W. Mykian*	5.00
____ PALMISTRY MADE EASY *Fred Gettings*	5.00
____ PALMISTRY MADE PRACTICAL *Elizabeth Daniels Squire*	7.00
____ PALMISTRY SECRETS REVEALED *Henry Frith*	4.00
____ PROPHECY IN OUR TIME *Martin Ebon*	2.50
____ SUPERSTITION—ARE YOU SUPERSTITIOUS? *Eric Maple*	2.00
____ TAROT *Mouni Sadhu*	10.00
____ TAROT OF THE BOHEMIANS *Papus*	7.00
____ WAYS TO SELF-REALIZATION *Mouni Sadhu*	7.00
____ WITCHCRAFT, MAGIC & OCCULTISM—A FASCINATING HISTORY *W. B. Crow*	10.00
____ WITCHCRAFT—THE SIXTH SENSE *Justine Glass*	7.00

RECOVERY

____ KNIGHT IN RUSTY ARMOR *Robert Fisher*	5.00
____ KNIGHT IN RUSTY ARMOR *Robert Fisher (Hard cover edition)*	10.00

SELF-HELP & INSPIRATIONAL

____ CHARISMA—HOW TO GET "THAT SPECIAL MAGIC" *Marcia Grad*	7.00
____ DAILY POWER FOR JOYFUL LIVING *Dr. Donald Curtis*	7.00
____ DYNAMIC THINKING *Melvin Powers*	5.00
____ GREATEST POWER IN THE UNIVERSE *U. S. Andersen*	7.00
____ GROW RICH WHILE YOU SLEEP *Ben Sweetland*	8.00
____ GROW RICH WITH YOUR MILLION DOLLAR MIND *Brian Adams*	7.00
____ GROWTH THROUGH REASON *Albert Ellis, Ph.D.*	7.00
____ GUIDE TO PERSONAL HAPPINESS *Albert Ellis, Ph.D. & Irving Becker, Ed.D.*	7.00
____ HANDWRITING ANALYSIS MADE EASY *John Marley*	7.00
____ HANDWRITING TELLS *Nadya Olyanova*	7.00
____ HOW TO ATTRACT GOOD LUCK *A.H.Z. Carr*	7.00
____ HOW TO DEVELOP A WINNING PERSONALITY *Martin Panzer*	7.00
____ HOW TO DEVELOP AN EXCEPTIONAL MEMORY *Young & Gibson*	7.00
____ HOW TO LIVE WITH A NEUROTIC *Albert Ellis, Ph.D.*	7.00
____ HOW TO OVERCOME YOUR FEARS *M. P. Leahy, M.D.*	3.00
____ HOW TO SUCCEED *Brian Adams*	7.00

___ HUMAN PROBLEMS & HOW TO SOLVE THEM *Dr. Donald Curtis*	5.00
___ I CAN *Ben Sweetland*	8.00
___ I WILL *Ben Sweetland*	8.00
___ KNIGHT IN RUSTY ARMOR *Robert Fisher*	5.00
___ KNIGHT IN RUSTY ARMOR *Robert Fisher (Hard cover edition)*	10.00
___ LEFT-HANDED PEOPLE *Michael Barsley*	5.00
___ MAGIC IN YOUR MIND *U.S. Andersen*	10.00
___ MAGIC OF THINKING SUCCESS *Dr. David J. Schwartz*	8.00
___ MAGIC POWER OF YOUR MIND *Walter M. Germain*	7.00
___ MENTAL POWER THROUGH SLEEP SUGGESTION *Melvin Powers*	3.00
___ NEVER UNDERESTIMATE THE SELLING POWER OF A WOMAN *Dottie Walters*	7.00
___ NEW GUIDE TO RATIONAL LIVING *Albert Ellis, Ph.D. & R. Harper, Ph.D.*	7.00
___ PSYCHO-CYBERNETICS *Maxwell Maltz, M.D.*	7.00
___ PSYCHOLOGY OF HANDWRITING *Nadya Olyanova*	7.00
___ SALES CYBERNETICS *Brian Adams*	10.00
___ SCIENCE OF MIND IN DAILY LIVING *Dr. Donald Curtis*	7.00
___ SECRET OF SECRETS *U.S. Andersen*	7.00
___ SECRET POWER OF THE PYRAMIDS *U. S. Andersen*	7.00
___ SELF-THERAPY FOR THE STUTTERER *Malcolm Frazer*	3.00
___ SUCCESS-CYBERNETICS *U. S. Andersen*	7.00
___ 10 DAYS TO A GREAT NEW LIFE *William E. Edwards*	3.00
___ THINK AND GROW RICH *Napoleon Hill*	8.00
___ THREE MAGIC WORDS *U. S. Andersen*	7.00
___ TREASURY OF COMFORT *Edited by Rabbi Sidney Greenberg*	10.00
___ TREASURY OF THE ART OF LIVING *Sidney S. Greenberg*	7.00
___ WHAT YOUR HANDWRITING REVEALS *Albert E. Hughes*	4.00
___ YOUR SUBCONSCIOUS POWER *Charles M. Simmons*	7.00
___ YOUR THOUGHTS CAN CHANGE YOUR LIFE *Dr. Donald Curtis*	7.00

SPORTS

___ BILLIARDS—POCKET • CAROM • THREE CUSHION *Clive Cottingham, Jr.*	5.00
___ COMPLETE GUIDE TO FISHING *Vlad Evanoff*	2.00
___ HOW TO IMPROVE YOUR RACQUETBALL *Lubarsky, Kaufman & Scagnetti*	5.00
___ HOW TO WIN AT POCKET BILLIARDS *Edward D. Knuchell*	10.00
___ JOY OF WALKING *Jack Scagnetti*	3.00
___ LEARNING & TEACHING SOCCER SKILLS *Eric Worthington*	3.00
___ MOTORCYCLING FOR BEGINNERS *I.G. Edmonds*	3.00
___ RACQUETBALL FOR WOMEN *Toni Hudson, Jack Scagnetti & Vince Rondone*	3.00
___ RACQUETBALL MADE EASY *Steve Lubarsky, Rod Delson & Jack Scagnetti*	5.00
___ SECRET OF BOWLING STRIKES *Dawson Taylor*	5.00
___ SOCCER—THE GAME & HOW TO PLAY IT *Gary Rosenthal*	7.00
___ STARTING SOCCER *Edward F. Dolan, Jr.*	3.00

TENNIS LOVER'S LIBRARY

___ HOW TO BEAT BETTER TENNIS PLAYERS *Loring Fiske*	4.00
___ PSYCH YOURSELF TO BETTER TENNIS *Dr. Walter A. Luszki*	2.00
___ TENNIS FOR BEGINNERS *Dr. H. A. Murray*	2.00
___ TENNIS MADE EASY *Joel Brecheen*	5.00
___ WEEKEND TENNIS—HOW TO HAVE FUN & WIN AT THE SAME TIME *Bill Talbert*	3.00

WILSHIRE PET LIBRARY

___ DOG TRAINING MADE EASY & FUN *John W. Kellogg*	5.00
___ HOW TO BRING UP YOUR PET DOG *Kurt Unkelbach*	2.00
___ HOW TO RAISE & TRAIN YOUR PUPPY *Jeff Griffen*	5.00

The books listed above can be obtained from your book dealer or directly from Melvin Powers. When ordering, please remit $2.00 postage for the first book and $1.00 for each additional book.

Melvin Powers
12015 Sherman Road, No. Hollywood, California 91605

HOW TO GET RICH IN MAIL ORDER
by Melvin Powers

1. How to Develop Your Mail Order Expertise 2. How to Find a Unique Product or Service to Sell 3. How to Make Money with Classified Ads 4. How to Make Money with Display Ads 5. The Unlimited Potential for Making Money with Direct Mail 6. How to Copycat Successful Mail Order Operations 7. How I Created A Best Seller Using the Copycat Technique 8. How to Start and Run a Profitable Mail Order, Special Interest Book or Record Business 9. I Enjoy Selling Books by Mail – Some of My Successful and Not-So-Successful Ads and Direct Mail Circulars 10. Five of My Most Successful Direct Mail Pieces That Sold and Are Still Selling Millions of Dollars Worth of Books 11. Melvin Powers' Mail Order Success Strategy – Follow It and You'll Become a Millionaire 12. How to Sell Your Products to Mail Order Companies, Retail Outlets, Jobbers, and Fund Raisers for Maximum Distribution and Profits 13. How to Get Free Display Ads and Publicity That Can Put You on the Road to Riches 14. How to Make Your Advertising Copy Sizzle to Make You Wealthy 15. Questions and Answers to Help You Get Started Making Money in Your Own Mail Order Business 16. A Personal Word from Melvin Powers 17. How to Get Started Making Money in Mail Order. 18. Selling Products on Television - An Exciting Challenge   8½"x11" — 352 Pages . . . $20.00

HOW TO SELF-PUBLISH YOUR BOOK AND HAVE THE FUN AND EXCITEMENT OF BEING A BEST-SELLING AUTHOR
by Melvin Powers

An expert's step-by-step guide to successfully marketing your book   240 Pages . . . $20.00

A NEW GUIDE TO RATIONAL LIVING
by Albert Ellis, Ph.D. & Robert A. Harper, Ph.D.

1. How Far Can You Go With Self-Analysis? 2. You Feel the Way You Think 3. Feeling Well by Thinking Straight 4. How You Create Your Feelings 5. Thinking Yourself Out of Emotional Disturbances 6. Recognizing and Attacking Neurotic Behavior 7. Overcoming the Influences of the Past 8. Does Reason Always Prove Reasonable? 9. Refusing to Feel Desperately Unhappy 10. Tackling Dire Needs for Approval 11. Eradicating Dire Fears of Failure 12. How to Stop Blaming and Start Living 13. How to Feel Undepressed though Frustrated 14. Controlling Your Own Destiny 15. Conquering Anxiety   256 Pages . . . $7.00

PSYCHO-CYBERNETICS
A New Technique for Using Your Subconscious Power
by Maxwell Maltz, M.D., F.I.C.S.

1. The Self Image: Your Key to a Better Life 2. Discovering the Success Mechanism Within You 3. Imagination – The First Key to Your Success Mechanism 4. Dehypnotize Yourself from False Beliefs 5. How to Utilize the Power of Rational Thinking 6. Relax and Let Your Success Mechanism Work for You 7. You Can Acquire the Habit of Happiness 8. Ingredients of the Success-Type Personality and How to Acquire Them 9. The Failure Mechanism: How to Make It Work For You Instead of Against You 10. How to Remove Emotional Scars, or How to Give Yourself an Emotional Face Lift 11. How to Unlock Your Real Personality 12. Do-It-Yourself Tranquilizers   288 Pages . . . $7.00

A PRACTICAL GUIDE TO SELF-HYPNOSIS
by Melvin Powers

1. What You Should Know About Self-Hypnosis 2. What About the Dangers of Hypnosis? 3. Is Hypnosis the Answer? 4. How Does Self-Hypnosis Work? 5. How to Arouse Yourself from the Self-Hypnotic State 6. How to Attain Self-Hypnosis 7. Deepening the Self-Hypnotic State 8. What You Should Know About Becoming an Excellent Subject 9. Techniques for Reaching the Somnambulistic State 10. A New Approach to Self-Hypnosis When All Else Fails 11. Psychological Aids and Their Function 12. The Nature of Hypnosis 13. Practical Applications of Self-Hypnosis   128 Pages . . . $5.00

The books listed above can be obtained from your book dealer or directly from Melvin Powers. When ordering, please remit $2.00 postage for the first book and $1.00 for each additional book.

Melvin Powers
12015 Sherman Road, No. Hollywood, California 91605